IN THE STORM

IN THE STORM

BY

LESLIE F. CHURCH, B.A., Ph.D.

THE EPWORTH PRESS
(EDGAR C. BARTON)
25-35 CITY ROAD, LONDON, E.C.1

BOOK
PRODUCTION
WAR ECONOMY
STANDARD

Made in Great Britain

CONTENTS

my heart, for there is no time, still less desire, for finesse.

There is an old French proverb: *Toujours ne dure orage ni guerre*—'Neither storm nor war last for ever'. That is a true saying—yet is it a blessed thing to grow strong in the storm, and afterwards be ready to build again the City of God.

I

THEY SHALL SEE GOD

Blessed are the pure in heart: for they shall see God.

MATTHEW V. 8

My song is in sighing,
my life is in langing,
til I see my King
So fair in Thy shining.

RICHARD ROLLE:
on the Theme of the Holy Name

$\mathcal{C}$AN a man see God—the finite look upon the Infinite? Even though there be those who have thought they caught a glimpse as they brooded, in solitude, upon the immensities, can we who struggle in a world of blood and tears and stormy separations expect to see God there? Yet where should the Lord of Life be found more surely than amidst those who battle with death?

Maybe we shall not find our answer until we have put aside our little measurements of time and space and circumstance! We must learn, as Plotinus said, that 'God is not in a certain place, but wherever anything is able to come into contact with Him there He is present'. It matters little whether a man be in the storm or the calm; what matters is the state of his own soul—his very self. Whether he be fighting for his life, or meditating in some quiet cell, he may be conscious of the Presence and begin to see God.

In a world of materialism Jesus walked and talked to men. 'Blessed are the pure in heart,' He said, 'for they shall see God.' They heard His words and thought He spoke of their ways of ceremonial purification. A rich man must buy a lamb without blemish and bring it to the priest in the holy place; a poor man must buy doves. That was simple enough! Yet when they brought their gifts to the sacrifice they saw the priest, the altar, the glory of great walls—but they went away wistfully.

The new Teacher was so sure! Happy are the pure in heart! What did He mean? No ceremonial duty faithfully discharged brought the promised vision. Purity of heart is not bought with a lamb, a dove or a threepenny piece in a collection plate.

That word 'pure' implied that something was 'taken right away'. To be pure in heart meant to have a clean heart, undefiled; it meant to have a single heart, unconfused, a purged heart that became the eye of the soul which could see—God. But we have made purity so unattractive by concentrating on subtraction! The word was used by the vine-dressers. No vine would bear its proper fruit if it remained unpruned, but the grapes were the object of the surgical operation. The husbandman chose this and that long shoot to be taken right away. The suckers were pruned so that they might not rob the vine of its nutriment; it was not the plant itself which was removed, but only the hindrances to its proper growth. Its life was focused on to-morrow's fruit and, presently, the purple clusters showed its rich fulfilment.

Now, the emphasis in all this is not upon the negative process, but the positive purpose. Happy are the pure in heart, not because their life has been denuded, but because it has been directed to a royal service, wherein is a vision of God. Youth need not find life dull because of soul surgery which ends in limitation, but rather may discover the shining glory of sharing in the divine plan. Happy is the heart from which all that is unnecessary is taken right away—the pruned heart growing rich unto harvest. In all the storm and in the sunshine it develops its fruit.

As I read the introductory essay to *The Flashing Stream*, that brilliant work by Charles Morgan, I knew more surely than before what kind of man could see God. I found a modern commentary on the phrase, 'pure in heart'. In those unexpected pages I discovered something of what I am certain Jesus meant when He promised a vision of God. He who can focus all his lesser desires to one great purpose, he who feels himself part of one great continuing process and is willing to harness all his passionate endeavour in an effort to help on that process without self-seeking—he who, in short, has a single heart, pruned but directed—may expect to see God.

In his essay Charles Morgan writes of an old countryman who plants an acorn. He kneels and does the work with reverence, though he knows he will never live to see the oak full grown. It is enough for him that he is allowed to share in the process. That is his concern, rather than his personal enjoyment of the result.

The poet seeking Truth with all his heart does not pause to announce with a flourish, 'This is my find'. He sings of his search, and his song is part of his seeking. As we listen we discover Truth. The mother does not say, 'See, I have spent all this in training my children.' She does not keep a profit and loss account. She goes on with her task, without auditors, for the love that is her very motherhood. To-morrow her children, grown strong, will conquer the storm. She may not be there, but her love will be in the best fibre of their being; she has had her share in a divine process. Sometimes, as she struggles, unconscious of her single-mindedness, she sees God. That is why, in all her weariness and disappointment, men call her happy.

In *The Flashing Stream* one of the characters, Ferrers, says: 'Sometimes when you are awake in bed, thinking, between waking and sleeping, your thought runs quieter and quieter, like a still, flashing stream, like Truth itself without reason. . . .' But when that moment comes to the pure in heart they see Truth no longer needing man's little argument to bolster it—and when you see Truth, shining and absolute, you see God, for God is Truth.

I

Here then we might begin our discovery. Purity of heart implies singleness of mind, which is the threshold of vision. This does not mean that we shall limit our outlook. There is a world of difference between single-mindedness and the single-track mind. The remarkable thing is that the single-minded people have wider sympathies and deeper understanding than all the rest. Their purity of heart involves compassion unlimited. They live in such a way that all the outward circumstances of life are winnowed and harvested. They possess secret store-houses which are constantly being filled. The saints who spoke of 'interior plenitude' were conscious of ever-increasing resources. Their whole being was constantly renewed. 'Increase in depth and power of life is in every way more important than knowing so many things, most of which may not be so', says Rufus Jones. 'What counts most is moral fortifica-tion, sensitivity of spirit, quickened spiritual vitality, increased tenderness, and heightened power to stand the heavy and weary weight of daily toil and grind.'

The pure in heart show shining, youthful faces to a world grown old. From them all shabbiness has gone; they are renewed. 'Age cannot weary them, nor the years condemn.' This is no ideal dream. I have seen it in real life—the transfiguration of those who see God. That is why, in the midst of the storm, while the heart of London is scorched by the flames of war, I am still sure that no evil devised by man can blind the pure in heart.

A while ago it chanced that I was free on New Year's Eve and I went gladly to spend the last hour of the year with my mother. She had been frail and lonely since my father died, but she never surrendered her faith to the storm. As I sat in the little room where she lay, our thoughts roamed back over the years. Memory after memory rose before us, till there came a point where I could go back no farther. She stretched out her hand to reach the watch, which

Bs

she kept on the table beside her. 'It is a quarter to twelve,' she said, which, being interpreted, meant, 'Let us be quiet a little, now. . . .' It was very still in the room, as still as I think it must be at the gate of Heaven. I suppose the minutes ticked away; I did not notice them—mine only to wait in a great silence. I looked at her face. A miracle had happened. I had never seen her like that before, though I think my father had. She was seventy years old, yet I saw her as though she had been but seventeen. I was in the little room, but she was, as the Scots say, 'far ben' in the secret place with God. Presently her thin hand reached out again, though there was no need for the watch. 'It's twelve o'clock, my boy,' she said. 'A new year has begun. God bless you.' As I stooped towards that shining face I knew the Master had spoken truth when He said, 'Happy are the pure in heart, for they shall see God'. She did not end that year on earth. Why should she? She had begun it in Heaven.

That is why I believe that, in the hour when the storm is doing its worst, the pure in heart may look on God. That is why I know that the vision is more than a fleeting phantom. It brings with it great renewal, and when the shining light has passed from the face of one who sees, the heart is still radiant with a joy that does not pass. The land of Tir-na-nogue is more than the shadow of a dream. It is the land of eternal youth and they who, being pure in heart, see God, dwell there.

II

Now this great happiness does not come by wishful thinking. It is not the blatant reiteration of a single note, but the harmonizing of many notes. It is the direct consequence of the constant choice of right values. Jesus did not content Himself with speaking Beatitudes. He lived them. Women loved Him and men respected Him, even though sometimes they hated Him. That steadfastly-set face could not be denied. It was the symbol of remorseless love, the love which offered the breast to the spear and spread its arms for the nails and the Cross.

In the midst of the storms that sweep our little lives we too must seek to harmonize its discords. We do not survive the storm by running away from it; the winds are too fierce for such escape. We strive to harness them that they may fill the sails of the ship we steer or give us at times the music of Aeolus. All life submits itself to a final focus and the brutality of the neo-pagan philosophy shrinks before the rightness of divine love. This attitude summons resources against which tanks and bombs are futile weapons. They fall as a pebble from a child's hand falls on the everlasting hills. We gather these new powers of the spirit into a spear-point of attack, and before them the legions of lust and the false values of temporal power crumble and pass into oblivion.

Men have passed through the flames, leaving their burning bodies at the stake as they went on into the presence of God. As the fire has seemed to over-whelm them they have reached towards pierced hands stretched down from heavenly places. Through the worst hours of the storm they have seen, with clearing vision, Another like unto the Son of God. The storm itself has been transformed into a benediction.

III

When Francis Thompson, in rags and tatters, trudged down the Strand, he found himself pursued by the implacable love of God. Suddenly he realized a strange new harmony in all the discord of his life:

> When to the new eyes of thee
> All things by immortal power,
>   Near or far,
> Hiddenly
>   To each other linkèd are,
> That thou canst not stir a flower
>   Without troubling of a star.

So, in these grim days, I too have come to see the strange consequence of purity of heart. To such as become single-minded comes new sense of sight. In each deed they do, resolute and steadfast in their sense of the divine purpose, they find a fresh revelation.

It has often been said that the sinner and the saint may look on a primrose and both see its spring glory, prophetic of summer joy; they may both alike smell the fragrance of gathered violets, because these things do not depend on spiritual qualities. But the sinner misses the message of divine love in the petals and the perfume. For him the beauty fades with the flower. Did not Judas turn when he smelt the spikenard? Yet he thought only of money wasted, missing the glory of a woman's love ministering to her Lord—and his.

The pure in heart, seeing God, are not afraid, though they be storm-tossed, threatened, crucified. The impure in heart, compelled to look on the same tragedy, can see everything else but God. For them the storm seems overwhelming. Their eyes cannot pierce its black fury. The pure in heart, bringing all their thoughts into captivity to Christ, to Love, to Truth Absolute—standing close to Jesus—see God through the thickest clouds.

With what Ruskin called 'the innocence of the eye', Jesus looked on sunlit hills, on flowered fields, on streets in which the children played, and saw all things as creatures of the Father. The wheat, the water, and the wine were sacramental. Through a thousand windows the light divine shone from the heart of God. He saw, and smiling promised man the vision, too. So in the storm we struggle until at last we see. A flower is a prophet; a child an angel; a contrite sinner a fellow struggler; a cross a ladder to the stars; Christ Crucified, the Saviour of the world.

Yes, sometimes, 'when your thought grows quieter and quieter, like a still flashing stream', you may see Truth, absolute and triumphant amidst all the passing storms. . . . Happy, then, in such an hour, you shall see God.

2

STEEP SLOPES OF OPPORTUNITY

Lead me to the rock that is higher than I.

PSALM LXI. 2

Was the trial sore?
Temptation sharp? Thank God a second time!
Why comes temptation but for man to meet
And master and make crouch beneath his foot,
And so be pedestalled in triumph.

ROBERT BROWNING:
The Ring and the Book

$\mathcal{M}$ost of us seek refuge in the storm. There are moments when there is little else to do but to crouch in the lee of the hill. Yet storms endure, and he who would fulfil his destiny must climb the steeps.

The Psalmist cried out: 'Lead me to the rock that is higher than I.' It was not the whimper of a frightened child, but the resolute request of a brave man. What did he really want? The Septuagint version suggests typical exultation: 'Thou hast exalted me *on* a rock. Thou hast led me.' But is that the mood or desire of a man in a storm? To be perched on the peak of a rock, exposed to all the fury of the winds, is scarcely a happy position, however distinguished! Two of the great scholars of yesterday seem to come nearer the truth. '*To* a rock too high for me do Thou lead me', says one, whilst the other makes a change in the preposition: '*Up* a rock too high for me do Thou lead me.' Neither of them says 'lift me', and there is no suggestion of indolent expectation in the rest of the Psalm. Its writer is prepared for strenuous effort; the rock is a challenge as well as a refuge. A more modern translator gives a freer rendering: 'When troubles are too strong for me, do Thou direct me.' But the rock has gone! One misses it. In the storm that is battering the

world to-day, I have remembered a sturdy old
paraphrase of the words, and it has brought to me a
new sense of opportunity: 'Lord, give me a good,
stiff climb.' There is a brave and honest prayer that
hurls defiance at the storm.

In an hour when lies are bandied about as truth,
when sheer weight of metal is hurled against the
human spirit in an arrogant attempt to destroy it, and
when raucous voices shriek, too loudly to be convincing, it is fine to hear the intended victim cry out,
'Lord, give me a good, stiff climb'.

Now is the time for me to ask myself: 'What do
I want from God?' Is it a rock to which to *cling* as the
waves threaten to overwhelm me? Is it a rock behind
which I may *crouch* as the sandstorm sweeps past?
Or is it a rock whose slopes I may *climb* to a freer air,
a farther view? As a child I wanted escape. The
walls that were about me were restraining walls. I
longed, as we all do in those first years, to break
through into the mysterious, fascinating Beyond.
When I became a youth I wanted adventure. It did
not matter much what the adventure should be about,
so long as I might 'try my luck'—experiment with
life. The years passed swiftly, and manhood found
me venturesome still, but now it must be adventure
with a purpose—I wanted achievement. That is the
way it has been with most of us, I think. At first we
felt the vague desire to escape all bonds; then the
more positive need for letters-of-mark to go a-
privateering; then, finally, the growing sense of

purpose, the desire to attain. There was a choice of goals. Some looked easy, close at hand, over level ground. One was so far away it could not, itself, be seen. Only the fact that all that was best in one's soul responded to its magnetic pull, made one know it was there. Far off, high up, a rock wreathed in storm clouds, but the way to all that was worth while, yonder lay the true end of my life, but the rock was too high for me to climb—by myself.

So you and I have lived facing steep ascents either accepting them as another stage in our progress or cowering at the foot and hoping to continue our ourney in the valley.

To-day the Psalmist seems to be giving us his prayer as a pattern of our own: 'Lord, give us a good, stiff climb.'

Little systems that have had their day are crumbling. The world is tormented by a storm of power politics, which turns the nations into a pack of cave-bears snarling and rending one another. We are conscious of broken purposes and the shattering of dreams, and conscious, too, that in the hearts of many there is a vague kindliness and goodwill which fails to get results. In this storm I ask myself whether there is anything which can withstand the shock and do more than survive. In the face of all the antagonisms and infidelities, have I any sure and certain faith?

It seems to me, as I question myself, that there are great fundamental simplicities which the storm has not touched. I still believe in God. If I did not, I should be a fool to resist the storm. I still believe in you, my fellow men. That is more difficult. Indeed, I only believe in man because I believe in God and see my fellows as they might be by His grace. Finally, I believe in myself. That is most difficult of all. It is only possible because I believe in God and you.

The other day I heard two Yorkshiremen disputing shrilly in a Sheffield street. It was after the blackout time and I could not see their faces, but their words told me they might be any of us. One summed up his philosophy in a final sentence: 'Well,' he said, 'there'll allus be war while iver man exists.' Do you believe that? I should if I believed only in man. The rock would be too high for me to try to climb. But I believe in God, and dare to ask Him for the steep slope, for I shall not climb alone.

The way to that best goal is hard; the rock is high, but to resign the best because it is difficult would be, of all things, least Christian. That is an excuse no man who is following the Master dare make.

Many a century ago the Temple at Jerusalem was ravaged by ignorant Roman soldiery. The Holy of Holies was defiled. Broth of swine's flesh was sprinkled over the altars of sacrifice. It seemed that Jehovah Himself had been driven into the outer darkness. In the hills of Judea, old men whose faith did not waver, spoke to their sons of the God of their fathers. Whispering of the abomination and desolation that had befallen the holy places, remembering, too, the might of imperial Rome, they made their decision. The evil must be driven out and the Temple cleansed. They fell on their knees in the darkness and prayed in their own way: 'Lead us to this rock that is too high for us to climb by ourselves,' and God answered them. The glory of the Maccabees was won up steep slopes from which they did not shrink.

In the Middle Ages a young man became the centre of a gay circle in a town in Italy. He loved music and brilliant conversation; he delighted in rich clothes, even though he robbed his father's warehouse, at times, of its stores of silk. His friends only laughed at his peccadilloes. Francesco was a good sort. Who could but love him? So down the primrose path of dalliance he tripped, till suddenly the Voice spoke to him of another way. Standing before them all, he stripped himself of his garments, and asked only for rags for covering. Every one thought him mad. He had never felt more sane.

He must build up the ruined house of God at Assisi. Trundling a wheelbarrow full of broken stones, he prepared to make a beginning. The rock was steep, but he must climb if he were to reach the shining goal he had seen.

Down the road came a leper, shuffling in shameful agony. How repulsive those sores! How revolting that living death! As Francis looked he knew, immediately, what he must do. It was a new and precipitous stage in his real journey. 'Lord, give me a good, stiff climb.' He gasped a prayer and went quickly towards him, to stoop and kiss the sores.

A medieval tale, yet unquestionably true. The young fop, in his silken hose, thrumming his lyre and singing a love-song, would have passed with his generation, but the ragged saint whose heart was filled with love remains through the centuries, Il Poverello, the little poor man of Assisi.

In these more modern times I, too, have seen men face the steepest rocks and thank God for the climb. In a storm of desolation that swept over a strong man's heart when he stood by a dead fireside, and realized that his wife had been taken from him, leaving him with a tiny babe, I saw the acceptance of strange opportunity. As I tried to comfort him with the proofs of immortality, he turned and said: 'I don't doubt that, old man. It is the empty years ahead I fear.' Then we were quiet awhile. He made his vows, I doubt not. That happened years ago, but men and women of the great city where he lived have come to him when the storm has smitten them. There were others to whom they might have gone, wise men and true, but they came to this man because he had climbed the rock. He knew the way up!

I

Here, then, we come to the crux of this lesson I have learnt in the storm. We face steep slopes, we

see the summit beyond the crags. What shall we do
—cling, crouch, or climb? The times are hard—
desperately hard, too hard for me to idle, sheltering
behind the rock. There are too many theorists telling
us that civilization is doomed, and providing no
possible alternative. We have been warned that the
future depends on the result of a race between 'educa-
tion and catastrophe', and assured that everything
points to a walk-over for catastrophe. When
Mr. H. G. Wells tells us he is tired of mere optimistic
trumpetings which proclaim belief in the ultimate
triumph of civilization, I agree with him. I am as
tired as he is of such stupidities. I do not believe in
the ultimate triumph of civilization, but I do believe
in the ultimate triumph of God. We have been told
that 'mankind which began in a cave and behind a
wind-break, will end in the disease-soaked ruins of
a slum'. The only escape would be in 'the re-educa-
tion of the species', whatever that may mean. There
is a passage in Seneca which says: 'I have told you
these stories to prove to you what eager impulses our
little scholars would have toward all that is good, if
any one were to exhort them and to urge them on.
But the harm springs partly from the fault of teachers
who teach us how to argue, not how to live.' No
one questions the critical hour in which we are living,
but one does wonder how man can learn to live
triumphantly if he rely only on himself and his
fellow men.

Yet the world has had its Dark Ages before, and

the darkness has not mastered the Light. It is the philosophy which pathetically disclaims its need of God that grows hysterical. There is a passage in *The Fate of Homo Sapiens* with which one is challenged: 'Either the human imagination and the human will to live rises to the plain necessity of our case, and a renascent *Homo sapiens* struggles on to a new, a harder and a happier world dominion, or he blunders down the slopes of failure through a series of unhappy phases, in the wake of all the monster reptiles and beasts that have flourished and lorded it on the earth before him, to his ultimate extinction.' Our possible fate is picturesquely described, but is 'the human imagination and the human will to live' our only hope of deliverance?

One does not deny the fury and the terror of the storm nor the steepness of the rock! Indeed, the sane man stands before it, like the Psalmist, and describes it as 'the rock too high *for me*'. There is the key to the situation. There is a way up, but I cannot take it *by myself*. The highest hill Man ever faced was only about eighteen feet by some standards of measurement. It was called Calvary and on its summit was the place for a Cross. The Son of Man climbed it, and we who follow cannot crouch at the foot of the hill. 'Lead me to the rock that is too high for me to climb by myself—then help me to climb.' If only God would!

There are some poignant lines which find an echo in my frightened heart.

God wouldn't listen to my cry
God wouldn't even let me die.
I love Him; I hate Him; Is He there?
Why do my eyes grow wide and stare?

If He would only speak to me!
Out of the mist or the hollow tree.
What is He? Where is He? I am lost,
Like a lone butterfly, in the first white frost.

If He would only speak to me! . . . But He does. Last autumn I had an opportunity to take two little London children on to the Sussex hills. The stunted hedges had not much to show save passing October fruits. The bairns had come from the great city, threatened by the fires of man-made hell. We stopped, as the hesitant sunlight flooded the little trees, with its uncertain gold. One of the children said: 'Isn't it beautiful!' I answered: 'Yes, very beautiful.' There seemed no more to say—but, after a pause, she spoke again. 'Isn't it queer,' she said. 'It's all dying!' Then I knew she had sensed the deepest problem that vexes our philosophy. The prehistoric monsters of Mr. Wells did not feel that, but the child, bombed out of a little London street, had heard the voice of God.

Beauty in what seems to die! Love bleeding on a Cross! Yet I know spring will come, unfailing, to the Sussex hedge, and I know Love cannot fail, and Christ rises triumphant from the impotent grave. The Crucifixion and the Resurrection are more than

Cs

incidents of yesterday, they are the continual revelation of Love's inevitable victory. No rock is too steep for man to climb—with God.

II

Whilst it is true that the modern situation is too bad for us to idle, it is equally true that it is not bad enough to force man to surrender in helpless and cowardly pessimism. There have been those who have wallowed in despair, and taken an obscene pleasure in depicting hopelessness. To meet such an attitude, some have been driven to the extremes of apocalyptic expectation and to adopt what may be called 'crisis theology'. They have maintained that man has reached so low a depth that he is no longer capable of any spiritual achievement, nor even able to set out to find his God. He has come to the end of all spiritual progress, 'the nadir of the soul'. What, then, can be done if he is not to suffer spiritual annihilation? 'Many persons', says Rufus Jones, 'in their despair of earth, turn to apocalyptic hopes of a relief expedition from the sky to end the sorry scheme.' In the Barthian sense, there is now nothing man can do; it remains entirely a matter for God. 'Lift me to the summit of this steep rock,' says man, lying prone at its foot.

This is surely contrary to the teaching and attitude of Jesus. Even the harlot was to go in peace and sin no more. For her, there would be a steep enough road, but He bade her set her feet upon it and begin to climb. The prodigal son, hungry and destitute, came to himself, but he did not find his father waiting with a conveyance to take him home. 'When he came to himself,' said Jesus, 'he said, *I will arise and go to my father. . . .*' When he saw the familiar figure coming out to meet him he cried out: 'I have sinned. . . . Make me as one of thy hired servants.' There were other farms where he might have sought employment, and kept his shameful past a secret, but that would have been to take the lower road and live in the valley for the rest of his days. 'Father,' he says, 'I have played the fool, disgraced you. . . . Let me be a farm-hand. Give me a good, stiff climb.' In such a story the Master leaves us in no doubt. He believes in the spiritual possibilities of man—even of the man who has known the bitterness of defeat and suffers the consequence of his amazing folly.

III

So, then, we face the rock. We cannot be content to cling or crouch. It is impossible to climb alone; the rock is too high for us. Let us first make sure that the goal lies at the summit of the crags. The city of God is to be built on a hill, and life at its best is a joyful, stern endeavour to climb that peak. 'Thy kingdom come', we pray, and unless the prayer be base and empty, we pledge ourselves to aid its coming. 'In your patience you shall possess your souls,' said the Master, and as we look on Him we know that patience is no passive acquiescence, but active compassion—the 'suffering with' this world in all its agony.

Are we, then, to find no comfort on the steep slopes? Is it folly to sing, 'Oh, safe to the rock that is higher than I'? When the storm beats about as we begin to climb, we are conscious, as were Shackleton and his comrades, of Another who climbs with us: 'I know that during that long and rocking march of thirty-six hours over the unnamed mountains and glaciers of South Georgia it seemed to me often that we were four, not three. I said nothing to my companions, but afterwards Worsley said to me, "Boss, I had a curious feeling on that march that there was another person with us".'

In this day of much trial and testing, we need the intimate comfort of such companionship. I go to the Twenty-third Psalm before I begin to climb: 'The Lord is my shepherd.' I want to be sure of that, and I think I have learned, in the storm, what I must do to make certain. On my knees I am learning to say, 'The Shepherd is my Lord', and to vow it shall be true. Only when a man has decided to accept this Lordship of Christ can he learn the wonder of His shepherding. Then, as he struggles up the steeps, he will find the pierced hand leading him round the lee side of the rock. So they will go up together, the man and his Lord.

ONCE I saw a little child run quickly to a place where wild birds had been caught in a trap. Eagerly she stooped to set them free. When she rose, with flushed face, there was an air of completeness about her triumph. She had watched the tiny prisoners beat their wings in vain against the rough and clumsy barriers which shut them in. Now she saw them flying to the edge of the moor, exulting in their new freedom. They had not paused to question their deliverance; they were on the wing, sure of their way.

There was an hour when Jesus turned to the men about Him, and said: 'If the Son shall make you free, ye shall be free indeed.' More tragic figures than trapped birds, they stood before Him unconscious of their cramped, imprisoned lives, refusing the freedom He offered, shut in by the very walls their lives had built.

It is not circumstance which makes our prison. There is always a pathway through the storm. In the Bible there is much promise of deliverance from trouble, but the word 'trouble' often means 'straitness'. Life seems narrowed and constricted by forces we cannot control. Our plans are thwarted and our progress seems to be limited by physical weakness or by hostile human agencies. Even natural growth and development are hampered by natural obstacles. The common daily greeting in Palestine reminds us of this. '*Marhaba*—may you have enlargement,' says a man to his neighbour. The strong Hebrew word for 'salvation' means 'enlargement', and the name Jesus means 'He who sets at large'. Through all the changing scenes of life, man is seeking to break through the barriers, to find a pathway through the encircling storms.

To-day we are shut in by strange necessity. Our eyes are strained to see bread and guns, things very near, but we lose our vision of things that are far-off. The near-sighted soul is always depressed. The far horizon, the sense of wayfaring and the moral courage to attempt the journey—these things we need. Without them our lives are straitened and mean. When Robert Bridges reminded us that Rafael 'venturing to show God in Man gave a child's eyes of wonder to the Baby Christ', he said:

'Tis divinest childhood's incomparable bloom,
the loss whereof leaveth the man's face shabby and dull.

Such face is index of a shut-in soul. The man who escapes this circumstance cries out, with the Psalmist, 'O Thou Eternal God . . . I will obey Thee eagerly, as Thou dost open up my life'. He has found a pathway through the besieging storm.

Though all the world trembles before a fantastic Frankenstein—the attempt to incarnate national entity in a pseudo-superman—he who turns to the effort to grow up alone. We feel deceived, and despair in the agony of disillusionment. We think we are the sport of circumstance and, in our weakness, surrender to spiritual imprisonment within walls that, at the worst, need only confine our bodies. Where shall we turn for deliverance, to God or man?

Strangely enough, we go first to man, counting God less than a dream. What, then, has man to offer from his own resources? Only, it seems, a great negation. 'The heavens are empty,' he says. 'There is no God. There is no good and evil. We act on impulse and all our impulses are equally right! There is no Maker of Laws. The voice of conscience is but the sighing of the wind. All things are self-existent, coming by chance and meaning nothing.' Here is a strange message for the soul that feels the urge to go on living, yet is shut in the purposeless darkness of a cell! The universe is mindless, the grave is hopeless, the heavens are empty! Listen, then, to the best that man—arrogant, godless, hopeless man—can offer you!

> As I came through the desert thus it was,
> As I came through the desert: All was black,
> In heaven no single star, on earth no track;
> A brooding hush, without a stir or note,
> The air so thick it clotted in my throat;
> And thus for hours; then some enormous things
> Swooped past with savage cries and clanking wings;
>> And I strode on austere;
>> No hope could have no fear.

In that last line is, surely, the epitome of despair. What use to say to the soul in the dark cell, 'Be not afraid; there is no hope, in all the world for you'? It is a cruel stupidity.

The great negation has no answer to unfinished life; it has no intelligent suggestion for the future. It is itself a wall. It has no to-morrow, for to-morrow belongs to God.

In his arrogance and self-sufficiency, man some-times plans to break loose. He will cross ancient frontiers and sprawl over the earth, a ruthless con-queror. Blood and tears may mark his way, and the pitiful cry of the wounded child announce his passing, but he will open up his own life. He will hack his way through—and whither, pray?

As Victor Hugo thought of the Napoleonic course through a score of battlefields, he said:

> *Sire, vous pouvez prendre à votre fantasie*
> *L'Europe à Charlemagne, à Mahomet l'Asie,*
> *Mais tu ne prendras pas Demain à l'Eternel.*

We, too, encircled by the modern lust for power turn to the lesser, would-be Napoleons, and, echoing the French poet, say: 'Sirs, in your dream you may snatch Europe from Charlemagne, Asia from Mahomet, but you will not snatch to-morrow from God.'

So man is left to face the burden of the mystery either without hope or with God. There is no path-way through the storm save that which his Creator blazes for him, but that path is plain enough if he has eyes to see. 'I am the Way,' said Jesus, and we remember that the Way implies the wayfarer.

Now there is no sense in wayfaring if there be no Way's End. There was never any uncertainty about the declarations of Jesus. When He tells men He Himself is the Way, there can be no question about the reality of Journey's End. Nor can we imagine that He spoke to some section of the community which was not shut in by circumstance. It is a word spoken to all men—a word that concerns fullness of life, enlargement, deliverance from the dark cell. It lifts the soul above its fears of poison gas or deadly disease, and points to his destiny as an eternal child of God.

II

Here then we begin to see, though it be only through a tiny window as yet, the open road—a pilgrim way. Everything depends, now, on our reaction to the vision. 'O Thou Eternal God . . . I will obey Thee eagerly, as Thou dost open up my life.'

Here is a challenge to live, but it concerns the innermost life of the soul. The storms we fear, the walls that seem to shut us in, have threatened the body rather than the spirit. It is strange how much more real is our anxiety for physical security than for increase in spiritual life. As soon as that becomes our chief concern, the powers of the soul are enlarged. In the words of Rendel Harris, 'For those whom God

enlarges there is unspeakable increase in the percep-
tive powers of the soul'. We begin to see life fitting
in to some far-reaching plan. 'The mystery of life
becomes simple in the mystery of God.'

This is not to beg the question, for, though there
must ever be for us mortals the divine mystery, there
is for us, too, the divine revelation. Supposing we
said, quite simply, that the idea of Jesus opens up or enlarges a man's life. Would that be meaningless? The
late Dean of St. Paul's gives us a clue to the answer.
'One test is infallible', he says. 'Whatever view of
reality (or experience of indwelling power) deepens
our sense of the tremendous issues of life in the world
wherein we move, is *for us* nearer the truth than any
view which diminishes that sense.' When danger
threatens my body, or circumstances cramp my little
plans, would it make any difference if I looked at the
pattern life of Jesus? I seem to see Him facing Pilate,
surrounded by the bloodthirsty mob, saying with
voice so quiet that all the world has heard His words
through the centuries, 'My kingdom is not of this
world'. No physical brutality can shut Him in; He
is the Pilgrim on His way to Way's End. I seem to
hear Him again, when His subtle foes had set a trap
for Him, speaking with unexpected calm and still
more unexpected words to a harlot, 'Go in peace and
sin no more'. No cunningly-devised circumstance
could hinder His ministry. Before Him stretched the
open road—even when His feet were nailed to a
cross. When I think of the ways of Jesus, my 'sense

of the tremendous issues of life' is deepened beyond all measuring. If this be the infallible test, then here for me, in spite of all the storms, is the true pathway, the open road. 'Go where thou wilt, thou shalt not find a higher way above, nor a safer way below, than the way of the Holy Cross.'

In Laachen there is the burial place of many kings. The reading-desk in the pulpit of the royal church has a strange appurtenance. A crucifix conceals a microphone. It seems to me a parable. The gospel of the grace of God, the enlargement of man's life, was broadcast through the Crucified Son of God. To me life grows simpler in the mystery of that Love. Fetters may bind my body, but in the recollection and by the power of that revelation nothing need have dominion over my soul.

III

My spiritual freedom, then, depends on God, but my realization of it depends on my personal relationship to Him. There is no logical purpose in my life until I have established my link with the Eternal.

In the storm I have remembered that the Master took babes, born in a dark hour, and blessed them. We so often forget how He did it. Any other rabbi would have stood aloof, held out his hands, and spoken conventional words. No one can doubt the truth of the record, for it says: 'took them in His arms and blessed them'. A mere fiction would have clothed the incident with rabbinic dignity; this obviously true account gives it nobler garments—the simple majesty of Love. 'How did Jesus bless the babes?' I once asked a school of Lancashire children. At first they were puzzled, then a shrill little voice piped out: 'Please, sir, 'e 'ugged them tight.' He was poorly clad, for times were bad and food was scarce, but no Poet Laureate could have given the answer in fairer words.

How can I feel shut in, if that intimate Love takes me in His arms! Wise men say the soul is shaped by the life it leads. When, then, a man accepts the Way and sets out, a wayfarer determined to reach Way's End, his body becomes merely an instrument. His will is directed by his inner self. The soul is the charioteer. He 'becomes the interpreter and master of life'. In the secret place he learns of the eternal purposes, and strives to bring his little world into harmony with them. He is no longer shut in though his body sink beneath a burden of chains. He is linked with the Eternal. The storm has no longer dominion over him. He has found a pathway and he knows it leads to his Father's house. There he will be at home, for there, surely, is Way's End.

4

LIGHT FOR THE LAMPS

I am the Light of the world: he that followeth me shall not walk in the dark-ness, but will have the light of life.

JOHN VIII. 12

> *Thus, when the lamp that lighted*
>   *The traveller at first goes out,*
> *He feels awhile benighted,*
>   *And looks around in fear and doubt.*
> *But soon, the prospect clearing,*
>   *By cloudless starlight on he treads,*
> *And thinks no lamp so cheering*
>   *As that light which Heaven sheds.*

THOMAS MOORE:
Irish Melodies

Ds

The spirit of a man is the Candle of the Lord, lighted by God, and lighting us to God.

BENJAMIN WHICHCOTE

O Thou, who art the Light of the minds that know Thee, the life of the souls that love Thee, and the strength of the hearts that seek Thee; help us so to know Thee that we may truly love Thee, so to love Thee that we may fully serve Thee, whose service is perfect freedom; through Jesus Christ our Lord.

Gelasian Prayer Book

*I*N 1914, when the world was plunged into the tragedy of war, Sir Edward Grey stood at the window of the Foreign Office and looked out through the gathering gloom. Presently he turned to utter these solemn and historic words: 'The lamps are going out all over Europe. They will not be lit again in our generation.' Twenty-six years later Lord Halifax, as Secretary for Foreign Affairs, went to Oxford to speak to the youth of Britain. Like his predecessor, he bore the same heavy burdens, in another war. He repeated the tragic sentences: 'The lamps are going out all over Europe. They will not be lit again in our generation.' No one who has known either of these great and good men would question their judgement; neither would they doubt their faith. They themselves would be the first to agree to this corollary: the lamps may be going out, but the Light from which they were lit cannot be put out. The Light shines in the darkness and the darkness does not master it.

There was a moment in the history of the Jewish people when it seemed that their last hope had gone, the last gleam faded away. They had been delivered from the hand of Pharaoh, only to find themselves wandering in a trackless wilderness in the dark. How could they hope to reach a Land of Promise from such a place? Yet there had come direction and guidance—a very pillar of fire by night, so that after long pilgrimage they came to the Canaan of their dreams. That was why they kept, each year, a solemn festival of remembrance: the Feast of Tabernacles, when the devout dwelt in booths of leafy branches, served to remind a later generation of the days when their fathers had no shelter save the tents they carried in the pitiless desert. There was a year when Jesus was in Jerusalem at the time of the Feast. He went with the great crowd of pilgrims to the Temple for the final celebration. The Court of the Women, the largest public space, was crowded at sunset. Eager faces were turned towards the priest who entered, bearing a lighted torch. Slowly he came to the great golden candelabra. Solemnly he lit point after point, until, in the gathering dusk, tiny flames shone out, symbolic of that other symbol, the pillar of fire that had led their fathers from the wilderness to the fair land Jehovah had given them.

As Jesus stood on the great stone steps, where He could see the people waiting tensely for this climax, He grieved for them, knowing the darkness of their minds and hearts. The tiny, flickering lights shone out, and the crowd uttered their thanksgivings. It was not quite dark. Yet such little lamps were at the mercy of a chance gust of wind or the pranks of a mischievous boy. In any case the priest would come again and extinguish them with the temple snuffers at the first break of dawn. The lamps would go out all over the Temple. The Feast would be over, and the crowd would wander again in a wilderness, without guidance of a kindly light.

Suddenly He spoke. 'I am the Light of the world,' He said. 'He that followeth me shall not walk in the darkness, but will have the light of life.' How many heard Him I do not know. Whether, hearing Him, they understood, I cannot say. But sometimes, as I have remembered the way it chanced that night in the Temple of David, I have seemed to see, as perhaps they saw, 'the light of love, which is for us and ever shall be the shining of the face of God'.

Who was He who dared to speak thus of Himself, in that holy place, before them all? He was the first evacuee in history. When He was but a babe, His mother had clutched Him to her breast, as she rode off, mounted on an ass, and heading south in the darkness to escape the soldiery of Herod. The mysterious land of Egypt had sheltered the peasants and their Child till the danger passed. Who was He? He was a prisoner sent for trial before a Roman, who was faced by a problem he could not solve. In the midst of the grotesque inquiry, the military guards took Him away, whilst Pilate considered His deliverance. The soldiers waiting in the guard-room were amused. He had said He was a king. Let Him be a king. One of them snatched an old tunic and flung it about His shoulders. Another, with a sudden notion, reached towards the pile of kindling wood, which stood ready for the guard-room fire. Taking a branch of bramble, he twisted it into a circlet and stuck it on the head of Jesus, a crown of thorns. It did not need to be placed neat and straight—better it should be worn awry. The rest of them laughed. 'Hail, king!' they shouted—then fell silent, they knew not why. And yet He looked so strange, so royal. Was He a king, despite the thorns on His brow and the blood on His cheek? Later they heard their own officer say, as he saw the Man hanging on a cross, 'Truly, this was the Son of God'.

Well that was who He was. He began as a child, carried by peasants to a refuge in an alien land. He ended, it seemed, as a condemned felon, dying on a cross. But something happened in between, something so wonderful that it gave Him the right to say, 'I am the Light of the World'.

As we come to our own time of testing, when men feel that the lamps are going out, it seems to me that He stands watching us, in the darkness, as He watched the men and women of Jerusalem long ago. I think I hear Him saying those very words to us. No other in all the world could speak with like authority. That is why I believe that if every human hope had flickered and died out, I might light my lamp again by the Light of the world.

In the storm I am learning that you can crucify God, but you cannot destroy Him.

I

If it be reasonable, then, to suppose that the way of deliverance is marked out by Divine Love, the world may dare to hope again. The darkness that is about us may be dispelled, for the first function of light is illumination.

When we heard that phrase, 'the lamps are going out', our hearts sank. We, who have known the splendour of light, shrink from the darkness. It reminds us of blindness, suffering, and death. Without light we can neither diagnose the disease nor prescribe the cure.

In a romance written by John Masefield there is a passage describing that effect on a young doctor. He looked for the first time on a West African town, lying at the foot of a river whose banks were gay with scarlet flowers. 'When I wearied of the glare of these,' he says, 'I had but to turn to the blueness of the harbour. I have never seen a blue to equal it. I cannot describe it, nor give you any effective simile; but if I were treating any melancholy case, I would try to send him to Little Massa to gaze on the blueness of the sea. If that would not cure him, what would? All colour must proceed from light; all light must proceed from the Source of Light, who is the only cure of our darkness.'

Our world, to-day, is surely a melancholy case, and in Him who claimed to be its Light lies the cure. Man's ancient faith has been challenged by a dynamic paganism and, for a moment, he feared that Truth itself might be in jeopardy. In vain, to rush a system of ethics or a godless humanism into the breach. No brave talk of social justice or political freedom could stand the strain and repel the attack. 'All reasoning apart from some reference to fundamental things is vicious', says Professor A. N. Whitehead. 'Every epoch has its character determined by the way its populations react to the material events they encounter. This reaction is determined by their basic beliefs, by their hopes, their fears, their judgements of what is worth while.' Here then man needs light— the light whereby he may perceive Truth, for without Truth he has no data on which he may form his judgement of what *is* worth while.

When I was at school I remember we had a kind of problem which was devised, doubtless, for some good purpose, but which produced in me a combined sense of fascination and irritation! A man set out at 8 a.m. to walk a distance of 38 miles 3 furlongs —perhaps it was those furlongs which produced the irritation in my soul! He walked at an average speed of $4\frac{3}{4}$ miles an hour, and stopped at three places for 35 minutes. What time did he reach his destination?

That was the kind of question which I was asked to answer. Usually I got the problem wrong. The reason was always the same—I had used my data wrongly! One half of our world is getting its answers wrong because it is using Truth amiss. But there is another source of mistake. Supposing my master had refused to tell me the time the man began his walk, or forgotten to tell me the speed at which he travelled. It would have been impossible to arrive at any right conclusion. The other half of the world is making its grim and tragic mistake because truth is distorted or withheld. In a philosophy which blatantly mocks Truth and exalts propaganda, how can it be otherwise?

The world is sick because it has not established, beyond question, the things which are really worth while. It makes its mistakes either because it has not sufficient data or because it uses sufficient data wrongly. A calm and balanced judgement can decide what causes are worth while. When man has discovered these, and consecrated to them his emotions, his passions, his desires—when he steps out, conscious of a great final purpose, guided by reason, propelled by emotion, illumined by faith—then will he throw off his dread disease and grow into the fullness of his proper stature, in peace and joy.

But this new life cannot come with partial Truth, nor can it be unrelated to some coherent plan. That is why man needs the Light which alone can lighten his darkness and make plain the Truth. Only the Eternal Son can reveal the purposes of the Father. In Jesus Christ there is revealed the likeness of God; from Jesus Christ he discovers the possibilities in man, and sees himself as he might be. Without Him, he feels at best a solitary wanderer altogether unconnected with the remote Being, sitting above the universe.

With Him he is suddenly conscious of belonging; he is
part of the plan because he is part of the family. The
Light of the world makes plain the relationship that
exists between man and his Maker. The flower in
the crannied wall is beautiful, but it is not good—
neither is it bad. As soon as man comes into contact
with Jesus, he knows he is a moral being, capable of
knowing not only beauty, but truth and goodness
too. He is nothing less than a child of God.

II

There is a further function which light discharges.
It illumines, but it also quickens. In the spiritual, as
in the natural world, light presupposes life. To-day
the earth was frost-bound when I went out. The
garden, tended by one who loves flowers—to her
they are heavenly tokens—seemed void of all bright
colouring. Then, in a forgotten corner, by a dust-
bin, she discovered a single primrose. Above the ice
it reared its pale but triumphant head. No rich soil,
nothing but a little patch of earth and cinders—
nothing except light! Only the light reveals the
destiny of the seed; only the light quickens the dor-
mant life and brings it to full glory.

I believe these things in the garden and the hedge-
row, but I am too often reluctant to accept such
possibilities for the soul. The moral urge in man is
quickened by every conscious contact with the
Divine.

I met a man the other day who had been a brilliant

scientist. His research work was known all over Europe. Two years in a concentration camp had almost destroyed him physically. He shook from head to foot, his jaw had been broken, and he had become an epileptic. As I learned the story of his sufferings I expected to hear him pour out maledictions on those who had caused them. Instead, he said, speaking with great difficulty, 'Oh, sir, . . . I want to get well . . . to go on with my work.' His work, incidentally, was not for the destruction of men, but for the alleviation of their distresses. That irresistible urge which triumphs over the cruder and primitive spirit of revenge and calls the soul to its high destiny when the body is broken and helpless is not of ourselves, but of God. It is quickened by contact with the Divine.

In the storm we are apt to doubt the benevolence of God. Why does He not stay its fury, or destroy the concentration camp? Why does He not stop war and the evils which men suffer? In such moments of questioning let us remember that God does not begin wars or build concentration camps. He makes men free, and He does not deprive them of their freedom when they abuse it. In the beginning it was a gift not a loan. If God broke His promises, how could I believe in Him? The law of God is an essential part of the love of God. If He suspended physical laws, the world would be impossible to live in; if moral and spiritual laws were intermittent and erratic, life would be an insane and purposeless existence. We learn that it must be established within the heart of man, and the love which comes with the knowledge quickens what is eternal within us. We know, then, that to avenge our suffering is a primitive and bestial thing, but to endure triumphantly and strive to go on with one's work is our highest destiny. Evil must be restrained, if need be by force, but force alone does nothing to cure the cause of evil. There is a moral factor which ensures that force shall be under judicial control and, being used to restrain aggression, fulfils its purpose. Thereafter comes the positive task of bringing to new life man's better impulses and directing them to God's intended goal. This sense the Light of all the world quickens within us.

III

Marcus Aurelius saw man as a little soul carrying a corpse, but Plato, with deeper understanding, saw him as a charioteer. Jesus comes to convince him that he is a son.

Many years ago Robert Buchanan was spoken of as the poet of revolt. Amongst his poems was one which described with poignancy the life of Jesus— and showed Him as a mysterious but pallid failure. It ended with the story of the Cross:

> The light shone out of the skies
>   And struck the cross on the hill;
> And Jesus moaned and opened His eyes
>   And the heart of the world stood still.

Why did Robert Buchanan include the light? In his philosophy the skies should have been in utter darkness, but there was that which would not be denied. The light always shines out of the skies, and man sees it as he looks towards that Cross.

In this winter that has gripped the earth, men in whose hearts the Light has shined will see the coming of new spring. They will rejoice in its increasing brightness, grow surer of their way, be conscious of the quickening of life within them. As Percy W. A. Izzard says: 'We have set our hearts on spring; our hopes are planted there with the more poignant eagerness because of this double darkness of war.' When Thoreau looked on the new, enduring light over Walden, he said that in such a light there is no room for evil. So we say when the Light that never was on sea or land, the Light of all the world, dawns in man's soul.

The lamps may be going out, but they shall be lit again in your heart from the Light that does not fail. Darkness cannot master that Light.

Above the edge of dark appear the lances of the Sun;

.   .   .   .   .

There's something happy on the way,
And God sends love to you!

HENRY VAN DYKE

On a very grey day I walked down an ordinary street going to an ordinary task with no great enthusiasm. Ahead of me was a small boy, whistling as though all the world was listening—or nobody! He was an errand-boy, going about his work very quickly! The rhythm of his music made me walk faster. Presently he burst into song. I drew nearer to hear the words he sang. Perhaps all errand-boys in London were singing that song just then, but none could have sung it more gaily than he:

> I'm not a millionaire
> But I'm rich beyond compare,
> 'Cos I've got a pocketful of dreams.

I almost began to sing too. The tempo of life had quickened for me—because I heard the grocer's boy singing! I wondered what his dreams might be in this mad world. Then I fell to thinking of my own, for a man should scorn to admit that hard times have shattered his dreams. True, the world was sore-wounded, war and poverty had come back again because of the folly of man. Would it be right to give house-room to a dream? Should not our minds be held to present production, to military strategy, or to

Es

why I am sure a man should face the storm with a pocketful of dreams.

It is not only that to set out on a journey without having a goal is to wander like a tramp instead of marching bravely like a pilgrim. There are those who would answer that a dream is very well for a summer day, but that in the time of storm a man should bend all his energies to fighting the tempest and getting through. That is one of the reasons why he needs a dream. Why should one fight the storm if it is merely to continue to exist? Give a man a sense of his mission, rebaptize him with the fires of the Spirit, set his hopes and his desires on the achievement of a splendid purpose, and he will be more than a match for bad weather. That is, in itself, some justification for refusing to surrender such dreams as keep before me high purposes.

But I have learned that God had a dream for me. Because of that He sent His Son to show me what man might become if, in his amazing freedom, he set himself to realize the dream of God. That poor fisherman who loved the Master so greatly, yet made such grievous mistakes, might well have said his dream was ended. Do you remember how Jesus dealt with him? 'Simon, Simon, behold Satan hath desired to have you that he may sift you as wheat: But I have prayed for thee, that thy faith fail not: and when thou art converted, strengthen thy brethren.' So Simon clung to his dream of becoming Peter the Rock, and struggled on.

We all fail, but we are not all failures! 'The successful people', says Frank Crane, 'are those who know how to make the best of it, to fall forward, and to manage so that when they stumble they stumble towards their goal.' It is the men who have surrendered their dream who 'fall all of a heap' and lie prone on the field. Remote as the Kingdom may seem to me as I struggle in this world of storms, it is an amazing thing to hear the voice of its King saying: 'But I have prayed for thee, that thy faith fail not.' It makes me certain that God has His dream of what even I may become in the eternal scheme of things. Because I believe that, I dare not let go my dream. I know that my goal is to realize, in my dream and my life, the dream and purpose of God. So I learn that I must struggle on and that, with such an end before me, I shall need all the resources of Heaven.

In that mood I come back to Jesus, who, in as grim a world as mine, realized in His own earthly life the dream. What was the source from which, in the days of His flesh, He gathered strength to endure and to conquer? I think the disciples often asked themselves that question. They had seen Him go apart into desert places, and they had sometimes been commanded to leave Him in solitude. There were times, however, when they evidently knew that He was in mysterious communion with God. Perhaps they crept nearer to Him in the shadow of the rocks. Maybe they heard the words He said. What would they think as they heard Him pray for veins can look for such an issue, because it refuses to acknowledge the possibility of being changed from one group to another. If the dividing line which separates one part of mankind from the other be biological, then, as Dr. E. L. Allen suggests, the idea of conversion is ruled out. The strange theory of Nazism condemns half humanity to perpetual serfdom. That very theory would shatter my dream. I cling to the vision because it is of a Kingdom which is a family. I believe in it because I believe we are all potential children of God—that is to say, I believe in God the Father.

Strangely enough, the day I met my errand-boy with his pocketful of dreams I heard more music in a London street. It was a busy shopping centre and the crowds were bustling about the Saturday shops. As I stood a moment waiting, I found myself subconsciously changing my attitude to life again. There was music in the air, and there was something strange about it. The fret and impatience seemed to be passed and I was carried above the little worries of the moment. We looked to see where the song came from, for it was a sound of men's voices, not strong but intensely wistful. Down the street, walking in the gutter, they came—six blind men, tapping with their white sticks, and singing. I asked what the song might be, for in the distance I could not plainly hear its words. 'I've found a garden in Granada'—that was what they sang, those sightless men, singing for coppers, in the middle of a world war. As I came nearer to them, I saw they were not sad. I wondered if they were thinking about the words at all. The tune was a Hungarian folk melody; the words were fitted to it, words that took one to the stately gardens of Spain, long ago. Was it all a mockery that men should walk in blindness, singing such a song? If I did not believe that the spiritual is indestructible, if I did not believe that God was our Father, I should surrender my dream. There would be no garden which blind men should presently see. But, as it is, I have the right, as they have, to expect a Fatherly love when I have entered into the proper relationship of a son. I believe in a Being capable of establishing and maintaining the reign of law, but because Jesus, wiser than all the wisest of men, said, 'When ye pray, say "Our Father" ', I believe in that Being establishing a reign of love. In the midst of the storm I can kneel and say, 'Thy Kingdom come', and as I pray I can know that in the heart of God there is a dream of foes forgiven and hearts changed.

III

I have a friend whose small boy was about to kneel and say his bed-time prayer. First he turned to his father and said: 'Now, Daddy, I'll say my prayers, but first put Teddy away, 'cos he doesn't understand this part of it.' The remorseless logic of childhood will not be denied! The tragedy of to-day is not merely that men do not pray, but that they do not

6

THROUGH HIS EYES

And when Jesus came to the place, he looked up, and saw him, and said unto him, Zaccheus, make haste, and come down; for to-day I must abide at thy house.

LUKE XIX. 5

In the story of Zaccheus—the little man who climbed a tree—there is a passage so strangely beautiful that men have easily missed it. They have written many pages about the kind of tree and have almost forgotten what happened there. 'And when Jesus came to the place, he looked up, and saw him.' So runs the account in the Gospel according to St. Luke. The revisers, doubtless for some good reason, omit these words: 'and saw him'. It might be argued, I suppose, that whenever Jesus looked He saw, yet I can ill spare that reminder.

Nor do I want to forget that He looked *up*. God has come down so far to look up at Zaccheus and me. These are not little, unimportant things. They seem to me the beginning of my search for Reality as Jesus found it on a day when the clouds were gathering about Him.

The road to Jericho, men say, was fringed with trees. The busy town came to an end in an open garden and a long avenue of trees. Pilgrims on their way to Jerusalem came happily to Jericho before they began the last stage of their journey.

This day Jericho came out to meet them. There were strange stories in the market-place of a young Galilean having raised a man from the dead. The more credulous set out to see Him; He was sure to be with the crowd. Even the more sceptical were inclined to join them, for it was said that He had given sight to the old blind beggars of their own town.

The road was lined with sightseers. Every tree,

one imagines, was possessed by the boys of Jericho, but one tree sheltered an unexpected guest. The boys in its upper branches looked down on a grotesque little figure huddled on a lower limb which stretched out above the heads of the bystanders. They recognized him—old Zaccheus, the tax-gatherer. What a chance to pelt him with broken sticks or ripe fig-mulberries! Oh, yes, they knew him. Everybody knew him and almost everybody hated him. What did he look like, as they gazed down through the leafy screen? They saw the little figure, mean and grotesque. They knew he was rich, but they despised him for his ill-gotten wealth. Everybody knew he had bought his office; everybody resented the demands he made, as he squeezed their pockets to fill his own. Zaccheus! The pariah dogs in the gutter were more loved than he! Perched on his uncertain seat, the lonely little man forgot for a moment their hatred in his eagerness to see Jesus. Surely it was more than idle curiosity which brought him amongst a crowd on holiday, for in that mood a mob may be most wantonly cruel. In his heart was some undefined, wistful longing to see this Man who gave life to the dead. Zaccheus felt dead enough! He had money, he had a little power, but he had missed life. In his heart there was still stirring a strange desire to live.

Fs

Somewhere in the heart of that little man, clinging to the branch of a tree, were marks of divine kinship, the link that might bind his lonely soul to God.

II

The procession moved up the road. Through the leaves Zaccheus watched eagerly. The people chattered; the pilgrims pressed on towards Jericho. Suddenly One of them stopped almost beneath the tree. The little outcast shrank into a still smaller space. Jesus looked up and saw him. Would He pass on in silent contempt? Would He see him as the twisted soul, dwelling in a misshapen body, treacherous and miserly, an outcast amongst men? Yes, He would see all that—and something more. He saw the real Zaccheus, struggling against burdens he had bound on his own shoulders and bowed beneath others his fellows had laid on him. He saw this unpleasant travesty of a man, capable of becoming a man after God's own heart.

The little tax-gatherer crouched in his tree, utterly unconscious of his eternal destiny. In his heart there was nothing but despair. For many a year he had seen himself only in the mirror of other men's minds. He had chosen his own path; he had only himself to blame, but now he was conscious of unspeakable loneliness. He was solitary, unrelated to his fellows by any bond save his selfish, unsavoury past.

In such a predicament men love their sense of

kinship with God. There is a charming story told by Tagore—the story of a little child at the fair. Wandering along, holding his mother's hand, he becomes absorbed in his surroundings. The colour and the noise attract him. He lets go the hand and wanders on, farther and farther from her. Gradually he forgets her altogether. The brightly coloured stalls and the noisy bands possess his heart. His mother, dearer to him than anything else, becomes dim and remote. 'At last it so happens that to find his own mother becomes for the child the most difficult task imaginable. The same thing happens to us.' Life's external circumstance seems to us the only reality.

Suddenly to this despairing, lonely little man, there come unbelievable words: 'Zaccheus.' It was certainly his name, and it was the voice of this Jesus speaking. He came out of the depths, half afraid that he must listen to some new condemnation. 'Zaccheus, make haste, and come down; for to-day I must abide at thy house.' Nothing could have been more unexpected; nothing could have been more decisive. This Rabbi whom half Jericho had been eager to meet was telling him that He was coming to be his guest. His loneliness was gone. He was a man amongst men once more. He was, in some strange, new way he could not understand, related to the scheme of things. He came down from his tree, and went back to that house of loneliness, knowing he would be lonely no more. It was six o'clock; the sabbath had begun for the men of Jericho, but for Zaccheus it was content with looking at it in helplessness or, worse still, in indifference, is a theory unworthy of man. It leaves us helpless in the storm, and illogically using spiritual powers of discernment while denying their existence. The men of Jericho claim that they know their Zaccheus and, despising him, leave him to rot or to continue to extort his taxes!

If it be true that there is a fair reality beyond the jungle of man's cruelty, if there be God's peace in spite of a forest of bayonets, if the Lord sees through the smoke of the temple incense and beyond the ashes of man's dead fires, can we hope to share with Him that higher reality? Only, surely, if we accept what men have called His idealism, and enter into that spiritual relationship which our divine kinship makes possible.

In the storm we learn that though the process of conversion demands man's self-surrender, its first step and its last, as more than one modern thinker has suggested, lie with God. He it is who, in the midst of the storm, sees us, not as we are reflected in the mirror of our neighbour's minds, but as we are. Mean, contemptible it may be—yet bearing in our souls the mark of our divine origin and our high destiny. Transformed, when we respond to such revelation, into men close-linked with God's eternal purpose. 'The real is narrow, the possible is immense', said Lamartine, but it is Jesus who shows how great is the possibility of man.

The hour is dark enough, the hearts of men hard

and heavy, but to those who look through the eyes of their Lord the greater Reality grows plain. 'The desolation vanishes away; the Spirit leaves its witness with us; the Divine realities come up from the past and straightway enter into the present; the ear into which we poured our prayers is not deaf; the infinite eye to which we turned is not blind, but looks on with answering mercy on us. The mystery of life and the grievousness of death are gone; we know now the little from the great, the transient from the eternal.' Those words of James Martineau bring strong comfort to the man in the storm. They will bear the test of his experience.

So it has seemed to me, in hours of stress, when I cowered like Zaccheus, hoping I might catch a glimpse of my Lord, He has looked up and seen me—shown me myself as I might still be—and, wonder of wonders, called me by name to receive Him in my heart.

The angry voice of the storm has been overcome by that Voice; the lesser things have taken their proper places. I have found myself standing before the Great Reality: God loves and God must care.

There is no other beginning of learning than wonder.

PLATO:
Theætetus

Old truths, new facts, they preach aloud,
  Their tones like wisdom fall:
One sunbeam glancing on a cloud
  Hints things beyond them all.

GEORGE MACDONALD

To lose the sense of wonder is to miss the deeper meaning of life itself. The man who stands 'cocksure' before a solemn mystery will presently go away convinced there was nothing to see, because he has seen nothing. 'There is no other beginning of learning than wonder,' said Plato. In the furnace of affliction, when the flames burn fiercely, the self-sufficient man, who no longer wonders at anything, will not find any bush unconsumed. The fire will destroy everything of which he was conscious, and he will cry out, 'There is no God'.

It has always seemed remarkable to me that a man on trial for his life should have reminded us of such a fact. When Stephen stood up before his persecutors to make his famous defence, he made no attempt to secure a favourable verdict. Like Socrates, he made his predicament an occasion to bear witness to Truth. As he reminded his judges of the ways of God with man, he spoke of the strange happening in the desert, of the bush that blazed yet did not burn away. Then suddenly he said: 'When Moses saw it, he *wondered* at the sight.' I think there was a far-away look in the prisoner's eyes as he told them, but how did he know about the wonder in the heart of that lonely shepherd in the wilderness of Sinai? Only because he too had

had been skulking in fear for years, back to the very place where lay his danger! It sent him to Egypt, not quietly in hope that the hue and cry had died down and that he might live unrecognized, but it transformed him into a deliverer, seeking Pharaoh himself and demanding emancipation for a subject race. It would have been a remarkable escape of gas to achieve so much!

There are others who say it might have been that the red sunset splashed the bushes with a fiery glory which deceived him. But the sun had been setting in such crimson splendour for forty years, and he had stayed with Jethro, minding sheep! One does not deny the possibility of these natural phenomena, but one does refuse to accept them as a complete solution of this amazing transformation. Something happened to Moses, something so tremendous that it changed the history of the world. He wondered, and presently hid his face and listened. The Voice would not be denied. He argued and pleaded his insufficiency. The Presence was there, would still be with him when he set out to face the Pharaoh. He rose up and turned his face to Egypt. He was God's instrument.

Is such an experience subjective? Can it be merely the effect of powerful imagination? If so, it is strange that it rescues a man from the fierce storm and sets his feet on the path to great achievement.

When Jean François Millet was a small boy, his father would often take him out into the fields towards evening. They would lie in the long grass near the edge of the wood, and watch the birds flying home on lazy wings. They would see the rabbits coming out of the copse to revel in the dimpsy light. Even the grass, swayed by the evening breeze, had its importance, for Père Millet was teaching his son to find beauty everywhere. Once the sun set with peculiar glory. They watched in silence. Then the man rose to his feet, bared his head, and, standing in wonder, said: 'My son, it is God.' The time came when the peasant boy answered by painting some of the world's masterpieces. As I have looked on the beauty of 'The Angelus' and 'The Gleaners', I have remembered that earlier hour of revelation. When, sometimes, I have seen a reproduction proclaiming its message from a cottage wall, I have realized that Jean François went on to know. It was God who showed him, in spite of cruel poverty, the beauty that does not fade. To a French peasant, as to a Hebrew shepherd, God gave a promise, a covenant, a revelation and a task. Both were emancipators in their way; both wondered in the Presence, and, listening to the Voice, learnt they were to be God's instruments. That was why the storm could never master them.

I

Now men wonder, at times, because they do not understand. Even the mechanics of creation are still mysterious. Man has barely begun his exploration, yet each new discovery points to a deeper mystery.

The poet of science, as J. H. Fabre has been called,

Gs

discovered new knowledge to-day. Can he now apply his knowledge so that man will realize his high destiny? Is he to be content with improving transport or making his body more comfortable or more secure? If that be all, he will remain at the mercy of any sudden storm of evil that sweeps across the world.

There is a mystery within. If he can relate that outer world of which he knows a good deal, to that inner world of which he knows so little, he may find a new significance in life. 'True wonder never ends with what we know', and the man who sits complacently and says, with an air of finality, 'That's that', may discover a leak of gas in a cracked rock, but he will remain an exile in the wilderness, not knowing God was there.

I have never forgotten an experience that came to me long ago. It moved me strangely then but I did not know why. One Sunday evening, in high summer, my father and I walked across the cliffs on the Manx coast. I remember I revelled in the uplands and the glory of the sunlit sea. After a while we stopped and, looking across the waves, saw the Irish shore in the far distance. The sight thrilled me, for it was there some of my forebears had lived triumphantly. We went on our way again and, to my great regret, my father turned from the sea to a village, where presently we entered a little church. We took our seats and waited. There was a sense of unrest. No preacher had arrived. Some one surveyed the congregation, and came to where we were sitting. I did not hear what was said, though my father answered, 'Yes, but I am not prepared'. He paused and said, 'Very well, I will do my best'. Then he left me and went into the little pulpit to preach. They were a congregation of simple country folk. It was a warm summer evening and I had resented breaking off our pleasant walk. The pitch-pine pews were hot, the harmonium was wheezy and the whole place seemed bare and grim. Why should I be imprisoned within those ugly walls? Then I was conscious that the restlessness had gone from the people; there was a feeling of urgent expectation; something was surely going to happen. The old Book was open—wide open—even I could understand. The quiet evening light fell across it as my father preached. It seemed to me that men were forgetting to breathe as they listened. Their faces were tense and eager; then the light seemed to fall on them—or was it another light? The sermon ended, and the congregation seemed to relax with a sharp intake of breath that sounded like an Amen blended with a sigh. An old man said, 'God bless you', as we passed out. The people stood wondering, as though some unseen Presence were in their midst. My father and I walked back in silence, but in a strange happiness. No, I did not understand what had happened. I do not think I understand completely now, but I know that as I sat in the comfortless pew, I wondered, for it seemed to me that Some One had spoken to my boyish heart and said: 'Will you be My messenger, too?'

IV

It was Newman who said: 'A true Christian may be defined as one who has a ruling sense of God's presence.' But God is Love and to welcome to one's heart the spirit of love is to become a new creature. That first hour of wonder, when we stood amazed at something we did not understand, seems crude and elemental. We wonder now because there is so much to be discovered, and because God is so patient with our dullness, so gentle in His guiding. No longer is our reaction to the flaming bush one of amazement, nor is it content with wistful hoping, but, with the faith of a child in the love of a father, our hearts respond in love. Our whole life broadens and deepens. We are no longer creatures directed by instinct. We are no longer fugitives cowering afraid, content to lurk in the shadows of the desert rocks. We must be up and about our Father's business—the deliverance of man.

Sometimes, when the storm rages most fiercely and the darkness gathers like a thick, impenetrable cloud, I see Jesus kneeling, weeping over the cities of the world, and showing man the way of his salvation. Sometimes I think of Him remembering Peter—and you and me. When I see that through the darkness, I know the bush need not be burned. I must take off my shoes and worship, for surely God has come very near. Presently I must set out for Egypt. There are slaves to be set free!

8

THREE AGNOSTICS

I know not: one thing I know. . . .

JOHN IX. 25

They hear a voice in every wind. . . .

THOMAS GRAY

But first a husk of peace—a soundless calm descends;
The struggle of distress, and fierce impatience ends;
Mute music soothes my breast—unuttered harmony,
That I could never dream, till Earth was lost to me.

Then dawns the Invisible; the Unseen its truth reveals;
My outward sense is gone, my inward essence feels:
Its wings are almost free—its home, its harbour found,
Measuring the gulf, it stoops and takes the final bound.

EMILY BRONTË
The Prisoner

WHAT shall the artist, the musician, the lover of beauty do in the time of storm? Shall he hide his face from the lightning and shut his ears against the thunder and the wind? In the darkness and the tumult it is so easy to cry out, 'There is no God'. Yet there is a beauty in the tempest which he might miss on a summer day; there is music he may only hear in the storm.

The story of the youth who raised his sightless eyes to Jesus reaches its climax in his final confession. The healing hands had done their work; the agony of darkness had been dispelled. The young man walked in a new and fairer world, but the storm had not quite passed away. Evil men besieged him with questions. They maligned the One who had restored his sight. 'We know He is a sinner,' they said angrily. 'Whether He be a sinner or no, I know not: one thing I know, that, whereas I was blind now I see.' Here is a strange anomaly—an agnostic who knows!

Many of the greatest artists have passed through a similar experience. In a moment of deliverance they have seen Beauty that before was invisible, or they have heard music that was more than music. The rest of life might still remain vague and uncertain, but one thing they surely knew.

We lesser folk with whom they have shared the revelation have feared, sometimes, because Beauty seemed unrelated, and the storm threatened to sweep it away. Like a child suddenly solving one corner of a jig-saw puzzle, we were certain that was right, but the rest remained a jumble. One thing we seem to know, but for the rest, we do not know —yet!

A generation ago it was usual to think of an agnostic as one who lived in a vague uncertainty, refusing to give any decided opinions on life's great questions. He was the man who took cowardly refuge in the great negation: 'I don't know.' I was often puzzled as I thought of Keats and Shelley, of Schubert and Beethoven, each bringing to man so great and beautiful a treasure, yet speaking so little of its eternal source. Was I to believe that they were the unconscious channels of God's grace? Was I to condemn them for a cowardly impiety? Had they some strange problem I have never known, or did they, in the secret places of the heart, hold fellowship with God?

There is some artistic expression which is as definite and positive as the word of a Hebrew prophet, whilst some seems but to stand at the edge of the wood asking a question or denying a fact. That the quest for Beauty should be beset by problems in this storm-bound world is no great wonder, yet those who continue to seek continue, like Abt Vogler, to find.

But God has a few of us whom He whispers in the ear;
The rest may reason and welcome; 'tis we musicians know.

It is fashionable to disclaim fellowship with such a community of the informed, and many artists vaunt their agnosticism with an arrogance that is challenging to the Abt Voglers who remain.

The world has been too ready, these last few years, to assert that it has lost its faith in gods and men, though it still maintained a sentimental attachment to the beautiful. Religion has been dismissed with a shrug of indifference. Hero-worship has been discountenanced by an exceptionally unpleasant school of biographers, who have made capital out of what has been called 'debunking the saints'. Now the threatening storm has broken and the bombs have shattered much that we discover we held dear. Already we are wondering how we shall restore the beauty madness would destroy. But though bombs may break beautiful things, they cannot destroy beauty. That is eternal, because it is of God.

What has the artist, the creator or lover of beauty, to say about God now?

The answer depends largely upon our definition of an agnostic. Let us take the simplest, which declares that he is a man who says, 'I don't know'. There is a sense in which no true artist dare say that, lest he betray his trust. There is a sense, too, in which he must say it. In fact there are at least three types of men who begin by saying, 'I don't know'.

I

There is, first, the man who says, 'I don't know—and I don't care'. He imagines himself to be a carefree soul at perfect liberty to express, in his own medium, beauty without reference to its eternal values. In a discerning essay by J. H. Bodgener, there is this striking passage: 'Any element destructive of the uniting principle that binds the triad Beauty, Truth, and Goodness together, is, in the long run, destructive. Either the output is restricted, the range of subjects limited, or else, as seems to be the case, a blight settles upon the fruit.' Something is missing and, in spite of noisy denials, we know that the artist is conscious of its absence.

Some time ago I saw Epstein's 'Genesis' in Manchester Art Gallery. Next to me was a woman from the mills, a woman grown old too soon. She looked in terror at the grotesque and monstrous figure, then turned to me and said, 'My God! It's worse nor th' cotton trade, mister.' In my heart I agreed with her until, suddenly, I saw a likeness which startled me. The hand of the old woman and the hand of 'Genesis' were identical, worn and misshapen by the tragedy of motherhood without God. All that should have been sacramental and sublime had become a hideous, soulless mechanism, without purpose, without hope, without a trace of the eternal Goodness which might have redeemed!

There is in human life a sense of what Maeterlinck

calls 'lostness', but no true artist can leave it at that. In his music or his poetry or his painting he cannot merely portray the state of being lost without thinking of the possibility of the lost being found. When he shrugs his shoulders and says, 'I don't know, and, really, I don't care', he is betraying his trust. All eternal qualities are joined in some deep, underlying unity. The best within a man desires to discover this relationship. If he stifles the desire, and is content to display detached, meaningless fragments, Beauty presently slips away into the shadows. He has refused the responsibility of revelation.

Sometimes a man stands on the border-line a moment in hesitation. There is another statue by Epstein, a statue of Christ. He stands veiled with a garment that unveils. Here is amazing technique, but, if you look closely, there is something more. It is not the side which is pierced; it is the eyeballs. Tortured in mind as well as body, there stands the stricken Christ. Who is this Christ? 'I don't know,' says the artist, 'but . . .' How will that sentence end?

II

From this border-line one reaches that second type of agnosticism which says, 'I don't know . . . but I want to know'. Here one comes to a higher level. There is still doubt but there is also desire. It is, as sometimes I have seen men, unskilled and clumsy, making haste to bind up another's wounds and groping for the secret of healing the hurt for which their own hearts bled.

Some time ago I was speaking in Ely, and arrived an hour or two before the meeting began. A violent thunderstorm was raging, and I went into the Cathedral. It seemed empty. Even the great lantern-light window was darkened by the clouds above. Suddenly a thin stream of music sounded from the organ. A tuning in progress, I thought. The plaintive note changed. It became a wistful questioning that rose insistent above the crash of the thunder. Somewhere, in the darkness, the musician was expressing the hunger of his soul. Many things may have been hidden from him. One thing he knew beyond all doubting; he had heard the music that is immortal. As I listened to the note of yearning, I knew that he longed to know the secret place of the Presence which brings peace to all the world. I never saw his face. I had heard his spirit pleading with God in the darkness. It was enough. I went out into the storm joyous as on a summer day.

It is surely so with the Beauty God permits us to see or hear. It leads us to the shores of longing, and keeps us standing there, framing a question born of the hunger within our hearts.

Was it not so with Mary of Nazareth in her long months of waiting?

A little hand in the darkness
Was lifting the latch of her heart.

About her were clouds of great mystery, yet in her soul was no fearful dismay, no callous indifference—only the great longing, presently to understand and not to fail.

Such an attitude is often scorned as that of the dreamer, but it is the dreamers who cross the horizon and make the great discoveries. They are not content with a glimpse that hints of a Beyond. They must set out to see what is on the other side of the hill. Nor is it idle curiosity. The partial view demands full vision; the few glad notes must find fulfilment in a symphony.

Consider a tree. It may hold an unbroken sequence of life longer than any other living entity. It has a beauty peculiarly its own. The poet sees it lifting its leafy arms to pray. The musician, listening to the poet's song, sets it to the music that is in his heart, and the two together make their poignant confession. There is something more than the words or the melody can interpret, something more than poet or musician yet understand. 'Only God can make a tree.' The tragedy is that another may snatch the song and transform it into a foxtrot. A man may not know the secret of the eternal values, but if he does not want to know, he will be content with the rhythm of the tom-tom when he might be listening to the music of the spheres.

One of the poets least likely to claim an intimacy with God was Sidney Lanier, yet how surely he entered into it. For him 'music was love in search of

Hs

a word'. He did not know, but he longed to know and so it came about that his song was only 'living aloud', his work 'a singing with his hand'. From what seemed for a moment to be agnosticism, he came to a rich, deep faith. I don't know. How can I, who am mere mortal man, but, oh, I want to know!' It was no despairing cry, but rather the strong companion of passionate desire. He was dying of phthisis when he sang:

As the marsh hen secretly builds on the watery sod,
Behold, I will build me a nest on the greatness of God:
By so many roots as the marsh-grass sends in the sod
I will heartily lay me a-hold on the greatness of God.

There is no trace of weariness or delirium in the song. Against the unlikely background of the wide salt marshes of Georgia, this 'consumptive' stretches out his thin hand to greet his Maker. When I have paused, baffled and bewildered, I have remembered that line, and tried to say with Lanier: 'I will heartily lay me a-hold on the greatness of God.'

Such men, in humble consciousness of their limitations, see life laid bare in its infinite possibilities. They begin, not knowing how Truth and Goodness lie in the heart of all Beauty, but they do not, therefore, yield the pass to what is ugly. They will not, for they are great lovers, and true love admits no separation in this trinity.

III

Even so, there is one more height to scale. It is reached when the artist, knowing his own boundaries, determines, like Lanier, to surmount them. 'One thing I know,' he says. 'The rest I go on to know.'

At first, indifference was banished by the great yearning. Now, hunger and desire is transformed into a consecrated quest. These processes are not always sharply defined. That does not matter. The pilgrim has caught a glimpse of a pinnacle, gleaming though far-off. He suspects the splendour of the City, though it be wreathed in mist. He has heard a faint, whispering cadence from the music that is in the heart of God. He cannot explain or interpret it, but he can say: 'One thing I know, whereas I was deaf now I hear.'

It may begin, as Filson Young suggests of Bach's preludes and fugues, with a shepherd piping on a sunny hillside, sadly, of the vaguely unattainable. It may change presently to a song of universal love, cradled in deep unrest. At last it may end in trumpet calls from the clouds, in messages of things changeless and eternal which speed our souls from one great certainty to know the grace of God.

In the storm I am remembering again there must be that sure beginning—God is Love. I find it clearly in the person of our Lord, and through Him in a new vision of the world in which I love. He it is who opens my eyes and ears so that I find unexpected beauty—in primroses and a blackbird's song, in Bach and the poet of Dove Cottage:

> 'Let there be life,' said God. And what He wrought
> Went past, in myriad marching lives, and brought
> This hour, this quiet room, and my small thought
> Holding invisible vastness in His hands.

A man may know that quiet room, but he need not find it empty.

'I have been so blind,' says youth. 'One thing I know—I see.' 'I have been so deaf,' says Mary in the garden near the tomb. 'One thing I know—I heard Him call my name.' 'I have been so disappointing to myself, so cruel to God,' says Peter. 'One thing I know—He prayed for me.' And, after all, we are men and women like these and, like them, we may go on to know.

There can be no quest of Beauty that turns its back on Truth and Goodness, for Beauty is but 'broken ugliness' where Love is banned, and Love can tolerate no falsehood, no evil.

So I come to nightfall, many a day, knowing so little, yet knowing as Jesus Himself taught me, that, if I arise and go to my Father, I shall find Him on the way, coming out to meet me. That strange adventure that began in knowing nothing shows me at long last the way Home.

9

DOG INTO DISCIPLE

And Thomas answered and said unto him, My Lord and my God.

JOHN XX. 28

What servant is more attached to his master than his dog?

COLUMELLA

Love betters what is best,
Even here below, but more in heaven above.

WORDSWORTH:
Michael Angelo

HERE is doubt that is born of sheer incredulity or scepticism, but there is also doubt that is the child of sorrow. In the storm, when gigantic and chaotic forces seem to oppose, it is difficult to believe what seems too good to be true. None the less, the very circumstances which lead a man to doubt are the circumstances in which tremendous faith may come to life.

It is strange that the most important things in the life of Thomas the disciple should be either forgotten or misunderstood. He is constantly cited as the classic example of the doubter. Usually he is condemned or reproached. Here is the man who would not believe until he could touch those wounded hands! This is not only unfair; it is ill-informed. There is much more than the contrast between crude doubt and reluctant faith in the story of Thomas.

As I have thought of the treasures that come to men on the wings of the storm, I have remembered this disciple and his astounding victory. It is stupid to condemn his doubt as the vulgar expression of an obstinate and materialistic nature. This man, whom we have too readily labelled 'doubting Thomas', has much in common with ourselves and some qualities we should be proud to possess.

There were, probably, three facts which made his

acceptance of Jesus as Lord and Master peculiarly difficult. In spite of them, his loyalty is, at least, as complete as that of any of his associates.

In the first place, his name apparently was Judas or Jude. In the little company of disciples there were two others similarly named, though they were known as Judas Iscariot and Judas, the brother of James, respectively. To distinguish him from them he was called Thomas or Didymus—both epithets that mean 'the Twin'. It was as though, at the very beginning of his new life, he was condemned to play a secondary part. (There is always a handicap in being known as Jones Minor.) The writers of the first three Gospels dismiss him from their story with the barest acknowledgement of his presence.

In the second place, it is believed that he was a carpenter by trade. Now, Jesus had been a carpenter in Nazareth. The other disciples were fishermen or tax-gatherers or—anything but carpenters. It was more difficult for Thomas to accept the tremendous transformation of 'a carpenter' into 'the Christ—the Anointed of God'. One might admire and love, but, after all, one had so much in common with Him. It was difficult to adore. Perhaps subconsciously Thomas felt some such restraint. Did he not know the way of a saw and a plane? Could he not judge timber? Could he not mend and make as well as Jesus?

An awkward name and a knowledge of carpentry may, under the circumstances, have been a handicap,

It is the devotion of the dog which is bewildered but which will never desert. No matter how unreasonable the way of its master may be, no matter what it may involve for the dog, you may depend on him. It is not a question of reason or understanding; it is devotion.

Do you remember the poignant words of Dr. John Brown as he describes the attitude of the old grey mastiff in *Rab and His Friends*? The carter's wife, Ailie, had just died in the little room where she lay in the hospital. James, her husband, was broken. For hours he and the dog had watched, hoping against hope. Now their watching was ended: 'Rab all this time had been full awake and motionless: he came forward beside us: Ailie's hand, which James had held, was hanging down; it was soaked with his tears; Rab licked it all over carefully, looked at her, and returned to his place under the table.'

So Thomas, understanding nothing of the reason that prompted Jesus, rose and turned towards Bethany. It was the Master who decided the way they should go; the idea of separating never entered his head. He was quite ready to die with Him—readier to die than to live, some have said, but, at least, let us begin by recognizing this splendid quality. It was not evident in any of the other disciples at that moment. It may not have been informed loyalty, but it was faithfulness that asked for no return. Here may be a despondent man, but here, too, is a brave lover of Jesus.

The old sea rover of whom Robert Louis Stevenson writes reminds one of the disciple. A fugitive runs towards him crying that the city and its temples are burning and Thor is being slain. 'Hurry, hurry,' says the man, 'if you would escape.' The old rover runs his thumb along the edge of his battle-axe, then sets off quickly towards the burning city. 'Where are you going?' cried the astonished fugitive, and the old sea rover shouted as he ran on, 'I? Oh, I am going back to die with god.'

There is something splendid about it all; it is the devotion of the dog, but it is not the faith of the son.

II

The next phase of the experience of Thomas reveals more strongly the part played by temperament. Dog-like devotion is good, so far as it goes, but it is not the complete expression of the man. He must presently know the wonder of a reasonable faith, but his progress towards this climax may cost him many a struggle. At times he may feel his world crashing about him; at times he may be filled with grim foreboding.

There came a new stage in the development of Thomas with the dawn of Passion Week. Jesus stood on the threshold of the last great sacrifice. His friends were perplexed by recent happenings. Dark premonitions crept into their minds. Just when they were entering into deeper intimacies with their Lord, there seemed to be the threat of final separation. He would take no precautions, and they could not understand such an attitude. Thomas brooded more than the rest. When it came to the last crisis, he would not flinch, but until then he watched and wondered, aloof like some obscure spectator of a tragedy in which he was powerless to intervene.

When Jesus began to speak words of comfort, he was, perhaps, impatient—almost irritable. 'Let not your hearts be troubled,' the Master said, but how could they be anything else but troubled! He spoke of going away, of leaving them altogether. 'In my Father's house are many mansions. . . . I go to prepare a place for you. . . . Whither I go ye know and the way ye know. . . .' This was too much for Thomas. He had been listening in the shadows and had spoken no word, but this was unreasonable. Where was the Father's house? How could he follow Jesus there? He had been gazing into the darkening future for weeks, and these words did not comfort him. 'Lord,' he began—and the very word showed that his devotion was unchanged—'Lord, we know not whither Thou goest; and how can we know the way?' It was an honest question. He had no vision of the stupendous issue that was keeping Jesus with face steadfastly set. The rest of the disciples were amazed at this astonishing interruption from the silent Thomas. 'Jesus saith unto him, I am the way, the truth and the life: no man cometh unto the Father but by me. If ye had known me, ye would have

known my Father also. . . .' Thomas was puzzled.
This talk of the Father's house—where was that?
This suggestion that he did not know Jesus, with
whom he had been month after month, in close
relationship, this Jesus with whom he fully intended
to die.

The answer drove him in on himself again. He
was not sulky. He was not querulous. He was just
devoted and perplexed. The fault, doubtless, lay in
himself, but he did not know where. If only he could
have seen a little more clearly! If only he could have
understood that in his Friend he could see the
Eternal, the Father!

Like many of us, he had unconsciously shut his
mind against the one idea which would have solved
his problem, the knowledge that God Himself had
entered his little life.

How dull is an existence in which one is continually
resisting the thought that the supernatural may break
in! There is never any expectation of 'the shining
impossible'. We must take everything into the laboratory to analyse. The tears of a child must be ex-
amined in a retort, and the light on a mother's face
reduced to a formula. How absurd and incomplete
it must be! How pedestrian it makes our conception
of God! Gone are the wings of flight that bear us to
heavenly places. Chariots of fire are merged in
omnibuses; suns and stars are vague accumulations;
we are earthbound, at the best but faithful dogs.

The solemn tragedy moved towards its climax.

Each day of that last week was pregnant with events that would affect the future of mankind. Gentiles came to see Jesus. A widow cast her mite into the Temple treasury and the Master was strangely moved. At a last solemn meal, He paused to wash the disciples' feet. It was all part of a problem Thomas could not solve. God was drawing back the veil that man might see Him in the fullness of His love.

As Thomas brooded over each incident, each conversation, he could see nothing but the death of his Friend and Master. That would be the end. No splendour of resurrection appeared to him, even as a wild dream. In such a mood he watched and listened and wondered. Was there some strange perversity in the conduct of Jesus? Was there—but he strove to stifle his questions. In peculiar loneliness, and with sorrowful heart, he dragged his feet from place to place, doubting the wisdom of it all, yet doubting himself, too. He could be sure of only one thing— that he must not leave his Lord.

The echo of those strange words haunted him: 'If ye had known me!' To know the Master—that was the unsolved mystery. To love Him—would love, at last, bring understanding?

III

Days passed and the Day came. Jesus was crucified, dead, and buried. That was the end. All the questions must now remain, for ever, unanswered. Thomas hid his face in the great darkness.

It was no great wonder that he did not understand; the wonder is that we, who know so little, have constituted ourselves his judges. What do we know about the human brain that is the medium of our thought? We are told it contains eighteen thousand million nerve cells, arranged in a multitude of groups, in patterns varying in each individual. An inconceivably complex system of communication links them together. From the day of our birth to the day of our death there is endless traffic over the system. As Sir Arthur Keith has said: 'All our experience is gathered from this marvellously intricate traffic, and out of these experiences we form our character and our beliefs. The brain is so complex that I believe it would take us five thousand years to understand it fully; and when we have done this, we shall probably be able to understand—perhaps to cure—every form of mental disorder.'

It was not surprising that Thomas, sitting brooding over his loss, did not understand the mind of God. That did not mean to say he must live on, knowing nothing, save that he had loved blindly and lost all. There were so many things he began to remember. There is always enough in the little patch of experience we can understand to take us the next step forward without fear. The moment had almost come when Thomas must face this fact. His doubt had never been an arrogant, intellectual rebellion.

Sometimes it was in danger of becoming intellectual despair. Thomas had to cease nursing his difficulties. He had to learn to see Truth and trust it, even while some of his problems remained.

> The sum of all is—yes, my doubt is great,
> My faith's still greater, then my faith's enough.

So it came about that he went his solitary way, aloof and uncomforted. Peter and John had seen the emptiness of the grave and went on to catch a glimpse of the glory of the Conqueror. Thomas, wrapped in gloom, wandered alone, hugging his memories, more precious and hallowed than before. They were all he had left—all except his own faithful heart. He did not doubt Jesus—but he could not believe in His victory. To know that he was alive would have been to him joy unspeakable.

His companions were accustomed to his moodiness. When he returned to them that sabbath evening they were prepared to share their happiness with any one, even with Thomas. 'We have seen the Lord,' they cried. He looked at them patiently, wistfully, but from a great distance. 'Except I shall see in His hands the print of the nails,' he said, and added with greater emphasis, 'and put my finger into the print of the nails, and thrust my hand into His side, I will not believe.'

There was no argument against such obstinate unbelief. A week passed. A shade of doubt crept into his doubting. His love, undiminished, was even more

Is

hungry. If it were only true, this strange talk of Peter and John and the rest. Their faces were shining as if they believed what they said. That next Sabbath he sat with them in the room where they said the wonder had befallen them. Then came the Voice, His voice: 'Peace be unto you.' Jesus was standing there, before his eyes.

He was looking at him, speaking to him: 'Reach hither thy finger, and behold my hands; and reach hither thy hand and thrust it into my side: and be not faithless, but believing.' He did not move. He could only cry out, in utter joy, 'My Lord and my God!'

That was his answer to the infinite patience of his Master. No need to touch those wounded hands. They had touched his heart, his mind, his very self.

The dog-like servant had become the awakened son. 'If ye had known me'—but he did know now. In a moment he had said more than all the others in that little room had ever said: 'My Lord and my God!' He knew the Way, and he knew it would lead home.

The legends say it took him far afield to India. He did not go easily. There is no final battle for a saint; he must always be learning. How could he preach the gospel to a people whose language he did not know. 'But Jesus appeared to him and said, Fear not; my grace is with thee.' So he went, without further question, a carpenter with a message and the unspeakable gift of God's grace.

There are stories of his building a palace for an

Eastern king, the strangest of palaces. When the king went to the plains, because winter had come, Thomas gave away the treasure to the poor. The king sent more money, and Thomas, with great joy, distributed it. It was not surprising that the king's anger rose, but the messenger who brought him the news told him that this strange craftsman ate only bread and salt—besides, he healed the sick and drove out devils. At last, returning, he demanded to be taken to his new palace. 'When shall I see it?' he asked eagerly. 'Never in this life,' said Thomas with great calm. 'It is being built in Heaven, of lives redeemed and health restored.' So the legend runs, telling of the strange deliverances of the apostle from torture and from death — telling, at last, of his glorious martyrdom.

Legends! Apocryphal stories! And yet, to this very day, the ancient churches stand in India, churches whose worshippers are folk of simple piety, wondrously kind to the orphan, the sick and the lonely stranger—'Thomas Christians'.

One does not defend the stories. It is not necessary, though somewhere in the Book of Life is surely written the record of this man, whose devotion brought him to the victory of faith. 'If ye had known me,' said Jesus, and Thomas, rebuked and wondering, clung desperately to love. So he went on to know, for that is the way of life at its best. It leads us into the deepest understanding. 'My Lord and my God!' he cried, and so began to know the Father.

10

HARNESS

Take my yoke upon you. . . . For my yoke is easy. . . .

MATTHEW XI. 29–30

He who prays and labours lifts his heart to God with his hands.

ST. BERNARD

Everybody in Nazareth knew the carpenter's shop. Indeed, its open door disarmed suspicion. There was no trade process to be guarded as a precious secret; there was no shoddy workmanship scamped in the shadows. The worst that the critics could say of Jesus was that He was only the carpenter of Nazareth. They did not charge him with being a bad carpenter, and there was no disgrace in being a craftsman. Indeed, it seems very probable that old Joseph had a sign hanging over the door: 'My yokes are easy.' The farmers came to have their beasts fitted outside the little shop in Nazareth. They knew they could rely on those yokes.

When Jesus had put away the tools and left the bench where He had worked so many years, He took with Him a wealth of memories. Sometimes in His words you may catch a glimpse of them.

The sight of oxen ploughing brought back those earlier days. He could not see the poor beasts galled by ill-fitting harness, without remembering the pains He and Joseph had taken in the little shop to choose the wood and shape the yokes. There was a day when He spoke to the crowd near Capernaum. On the hillside a team of oxen laboured. The yoke was badly made; their shoulders were chafed and the flies were merciless. As He looked at them in pity, He turned again to the crowd. They, too, like dumb oxen, struggled under a clumsy yoke.

The Law, with a thousand stupid amplifications, cramped their daily life. The restrictions imposed by the Roman conquerors were irksome and humiliating. The burden of their own discontent was heavy and grievous to be borne. Life, with its shining joys and heavenly music, was dull and discordant because they did not know the secret of God's love. Weary and heavy-laden, they stared at Him, as helpless and uncomprehending as the beasts of the field.

Humanity has reached a similar pass to-day. Bowed beneath burdens that are the creation of its own follies, it toils in weariness and often in despair. The madness of exclusive nationalism and the lust for power binds half the world. Social injustice has crushed men through the years. War and a thousand attendant horrors has brought men to an hour when they long for deliverance. No parliament, no battlefield, however honourable, offers them the rest for which they crave. Even the passing of the terrors of war cannot promise them the peace for which they yearn—the peace which the world can neither give nor take away.

To such a world the Voice speaks, as it spoke to the men of Capernaum: 'Come unto me . . . and I will give you rest. Take my yoke . . . for my yoke is easy.' At first it sounds disconcerting. Must the burdened add one more weight to their heavy load? It is natural that the weary should expect to find rest in the abandoning of burdens. Only as we stand with the Carpenter of Nazareth shall we see what He saw and learn the way of deliverance.

'My yoke is easy,' He says, and it sounds strange to this distracted world. There is a choice of meanings in that word—easy, kindly, good to bear. That last phrase seems to give the clue we need. The yoke that is well-fitted is good to bear. The oxen draw the plough best when the yoke fits. How often had Jesus Himself shaped the wood, easing it to the shoulders of the beasts, as they stood outside the shop in Nazareth! It was not the ox that was fitted to the yoke. All it could do was to submit to the fitting. Here, surely, is an amazing promise: 'Take my yoke— it is good to bear.' 'I will fit it to your need and your capacity, so that you shall labour without weariness, and find rest in the result of your toil.' That, it seems to me, is the invitation which comes from God to man, an invitation which is valid for the individual, the Church, and all humankind.

There is a sense in which the soul needs its harness, as does the body of the beast that draws the plough. I realized this one day on the station at London Bridge. As I sat waiting for my train, I shared a seat with a postman. He was very tired, but he had an understanding heart. The great crowds were rushing for their evening train, a little more nervously than usual, for it was wartime. Suddenly I noticed a little old lady, hustled by the hurrying multitude. Her years were certainly more than three-score and ten, and she looked very frail. I thought she was stumbling, and half rose to help her. My friend the postman restrained me. 'She's all

right, sir,' he said. 'She's going home from work.'
'Work?' I answered. 'She's too old for work. It's a
shame.' He smiled at me, with kindly tolerance. It
was obvious that I did not understand. 'She cleans
out our office every day,' he explained. 'She likes
it.' He smiled broadly. The little old lady had
reached her train, and was sitting back, tired but con-
tented. My friend, the postman, rounded off his
explanation. 'Ay,' he said. 'She likes it. You see, she
feels it's her job.' In some vague way I thought of an
easy yoke. If only each of us could find his proper
job! If only we were willing to be fitted with the
yoke that would link our effort with the divine
energy, and relate our most ordinary work to the
supreme, ultimate Purpose. I do not imagine the
little old lady had consciously thought of these
things, but as I talked to the postman I discovered
how greatly she was loved. I did not need to ask
whether the office was well cleaned. It was her job,
and she gave her whole self to its accomplishment.
She was very happy, even though all London seemed
to be struggling for her train in a threatened *blitz*.

I

The yoke is 'good to bear' because it 'gets things
done'. One might have said, 'because it is constructive', but there are times when the language of our
common life is more convincing.

The ox does not wear the yoke. It bears it for a
definite purpose. The loaded cart must be moved or

the heavy plough dragged through the stubborn, resisting soil.

'Take my yoke upon you,' says the Christ, 'for there are things to be done, and you must do them.' The man who accepts the rule and leadership of Jesus will be linked to his real task, as surely as the yoke was fitted to the shoulders of the patient oxen standing outside Joseph's shop. He will learn what things are worth doing and he will gradually realize how these things are part of one great process. More than that, he will find his own character transformed, so that he sees new possibilities and sets out to attempt what before seemed impossible.

Does this 'yoke' help us to get things done? To accept it is to accept the leadership of Jesus—that is, to be ruled and directed by Love.

Now, in the first place, Love is constructive. There is nothing mawkish or sentimental about its creative activity. The Apostles Peter and Paul did not languish on the hillside making daisy-chains in idyllic indolence. When the yoke was fitted to their separate personalities, they went into the midst of hostile crowds, and faced austere tribunals without fear or even hesitation. They helped to found the Church which has survived the buffetings and tragic mistakes of the centuries.

In our own day, while the storms bear upon our imperfect civilization, Love goes about its steady task and shows the most astounding accomplishments. The people who accept its yoke are the people who get things done.

It was not until 1907 that the Christian principle of forgiveness began to be recognized in the criminal law of our own land, but the effect of such recognition was seen almost at once. Within thirty years it had revolutionized the administration of justice. In 1935 fifty per cent. of indictable offences were able to be dealt with under the Probation Act. At the Assizes twenty-four per cent. of those bound over, and at the Quarter Sessions an even higher proportion, thirty-one per cent., were given a second chance of justifying themselves as decent, law-abiding citizens. Perhaps the most astonishing fact was that amongst juvenile offenders, under seventeen years of age, eighty-three per cent. were placed under suitable guardianship without the stigma of an official commitment. It would be impossible to estimate the value of this new method to the State, to society, and to the individual. In those few years the greatest war in history had been fought, and Europe had stumbled into a tragic aftermath. It was not a period in which one would have expected such progressive adventure. The achievement became possible because those responsible for it accepted the yoke.

On a thousand pages of man's history one may find examples of the accomplishing of things worth while by men and women who, consciously or unconsciously, acknowledge the rule and direction of Love rather than Hate. They based their judgement on spiritual values and scorned all personal reward.

In the second place, the 'yoke' helps man to see an

ultimate purpose in his toil, and to realize his present possibilities. 'Take my yoke,' said Jesus, and showed men the kind of work such yoke was designed to aid. The Kingdom of God is at the centre of His life. That was the supreme purpose of man's living. To accept His yoke, consciously and, as far as may be, completely, is to identify oneself with that purpose. To take His yoke means to accept His standards and, indeed, to accept Him.

It has sometimes been suggested that the call of Matthew the tax-gatherer was no sudden or fortuitous happening. In all probability, Jesus had cultivated the acquaintance of the lonely man, ostracized by his own people, and sitting grimly and desperately in the little customs-house where men paid their taxes with reluctance. It may have been that as He sat in the office He heard more than Matthew wanted Him to hear. A tax-gatherer was expected to extort the maximum payment from his victims. The surplus was his recognized perquisite, but it was embarrassing to Matthew that Jesus should hear the pitiful protest of an old fisherman forced to mortgage his boat to meet an extortionate demand. Why should it make Matthew so ashamed? Why does the mere thought of Him make all our meanness look more shabby? The deeds and thoughts that are focused on our own passing interests are seen in such tremendous contrast when we look at that life devoted to the saving of a world.

As soon as a man takes His yoke, he identifies himself with that dominating purpose. Like Matthew, he is ashamed of all the unworthy motives that would contradict it. For a moment his whole life seems too commonplace to be included in so vast a concern. He has come like the oxen to the street of the carpenter's shop; and he must submit now to the fitting of the yoke. There are possibilities in his little life of which he has never dreamed. They will remain impossible, unless he bear the yoke divinely shaped.

Men are discovering that great business may be transacted without fraud or oppression. It is possible to free our commerce and our industry from injustice, and to establish fair dealing in the market-places of the world. It seems a wild dream, but it will be less wild if you and I resolve to banish all mean and selfish motives from our lives. A new world order can only come through a world of new men. 'If any man be in Christ, he is a new creature.' There is a possibility for you and me—for personal salvation is the inevitable prelude to the saving of society.

The tragedy of war has taken its toll of man's faith and of his hopes. He can scarcely believe any longer that nations could live in peace. Yet that is an essential condition of the Kingdom of God. He who accepts the 'yoke' accepts the One who fits it to him. He may learn so to live as to make his contribution to the establishment of the peace of God on earth. It may be his task to destroy the evil that makes for war; it may be that he will have to endure the consequences of that evil. God fits the harness to his soul and it is good to bear, for it helps him to accomplish what seemed impossible, and to direct his effort to the ultimate and supreme end.

Beyond the discovery of new possibilities and the dominating purpose, he begins to find new power. Resources that he did not suspect are at his disposal. He goes to his task with confidence. His character is gradually transformed.

The world still continues in its anger and despair, but he is resolved not to be soured. He has a message of hope; he has a task and he must be efficient. Most wonderful of all he begins to learn that he can do the work! The world is frightened, though it blusters; he is no longer afraid, though he has ceased to swagger. Such defence mechanism is not necessary to cover his own weakness. He has become strong in a new strength.

These things happened to a little company of obscure, despondent men and women at Pentecost. Their experience is no fantastic fiction; it has become part of the history of the world. Nor has it remained isolated. That same yoke was fitted to the personality of a wastrel in Carthage, and all the world felt the influence of the work of St. Augustine of Hippo. It was shaped to the tortured soul of a German monk, so that he became Martin Luther, proclaiming to men the priesthood of all believers. It was fitted to the stiff propriety of a little Oxford don, and he became John Wesley, one of the greatest evangelists in Christendom. Countless men and women have accepted it and have accomplished great things.

There are signs that the wilderness is becoming a fruitful field, in spite of the storms that sometimes sweep across it.

II

A yoke, however, is not 'single harness'. The team of oxen were yoked together to do a common task. The Master Himself gives us the picture. 'Take my yoke upon you, and learn of Me,' He says, and so links us, not to one another, but to Himself. Surely this yoke is good to bear. It guarantees co-operative effort and each man's yoke-fellow is the Lord.

That is the final secret of this 'easy' yoke. No matter how hard the soil, how formidable the obstacles, how fierce the storms, here is a guarantee of inward peace and invincible confidence.

I have sometimes thought of that carpenter's shop, and of Him who worked at its bench after old Joseph was dead. What did His neighbours think of Him? One thing is sure—they trusted Him.

That lad who found his lass and was to wed her; they must have a house and a bit of furniture. I can imagine how the old folk talked it over, as parents do. 'We'll go down and see Jesus about it,' they would say. 'He'll understand.' They came to the shop and told Him. So He made the simple things that were to be the furniture of a new home.

Presently the young folk entered the house and possessed it. To them it was a palace. The day came when the lass looked into her husband's eyes and told him her great secret. His heart leaped for joy. 'We shall need a cradle,' he said. 'Let's go down and see Jesus about it. He'll understand.' They walked to the little shop and, speaking softly, told Him. No one else should share their secret. So He made them a cradle for the babe, as yet unborn.

The old folk grew older; they walked more slowly and, at last, their weary steps ended. They would not walk this earth again. The young folk wept, then dashed away their tears. 'Let's go down and see Jesus,' they said to one another. 'He'll understand.' So they came to share with Him their first great sorrow as they had shared their first great joy. His heart went out to them in great compassion. He did that which must be done, and they laid their precious dust in the quiet earth, to rest.

Life was no longer easy, and they were very poor. The bits of furniture grew shabby; some were broken. The neighbours would notice and sneer. Young folk got married on nothing; now they were rueing their folly. It served them right! The man looked at his wife and knew her bitterness of heart, yet there was no money for new furniture. 'Let's go down and see Jesus,' he said once more. 'He'll understand.' So they came to the shop of this strangest of Carpenters, and told Him all. He took the broken pieces of furniture and mended them. They looked as good as new. Even the most eagle-eyed of their critics would never see the mend. That night they remembered the years as they talked

Ks

together. It seemed that Jesus had shared so many things with them. His hand had made the furniture and the cradle; His love had healed their wounded hearts; He had mended the little broken things. He had made their house a home. How could they help but love Him! Perhaps there came a day when they felt it should be a temple. Jesus the Carpenter was crucified and risen again.

Forgive the flight of fancy. I cannot tell you the names of those two who learned to trust Him. I only know that it must have been like that. To be able to call in that strong, wise, understanding Jesus would have been peace to many a troubled soul. To be linked with Him in all one's enterprises—that would be an easy yoke, good to bear.

Whatever doubts my little perplexed mind may have, I remember in the storm that Jesus trusted the Father without question. He was utterly certain of God's righteousness. In that dread hour in Gethsemane did He not cry out, 'Nevertheless, not as I will but as thou wilt'? He was certain, too, of God's love. 'Consider the lilies,' He said. 'If he care for them, will he forget you?' In every issue He was sure of God's sufficiency. The devil might desire the soul of Simon Peter, but he was already defeated: 'I have prayed for thee, that thy faith fail not.' That was enough; the Father was all-sufficient.

How, then, can I doubt if I be yoke-fellow to the Christ? Let me be fitted with the yoke. It is good to bear. My harnessed soul shall rest in toil.

II

IDENTIFICATION

Jesus said unto her, Mary.

JOHN XX. 16

Many men are wise about many things, and are ignorant about themselves.

ST. BERNARD

Ken yoursel' and your neebours winna misken you.

Scots Proverb

And he said, Thy name shall be called no more Jacob [the supplanter] but Israel [prince of God].

GENESIS XXXII. 28

*I*N the storm some men are lost, but, strangely enough, some find themselves. The challenge of tragic necessity, the stripping away of all one's props and shelters, even the flooding of one's heart with the sorrow of a great loss—these experiences are revealing. In such an hour man may see himself for the first time, and the identification is the beginning of new understanding.

Something like that happened in the garden of the tomb on the first Easter morning.

Before the break of day Mary of Magdala stole out from the house of sorrow, where her friends lay still stupefied by the disaster that had befallen them. Their silent, inconsolable grief had been too much for her. She could not sit inactive; she must do something. But what can one do for the dead? At least she might assure herself once more that the sweet herbs were in their place. Hurrying to the open tomb, she wept bitterly. She would find nothing there but that dead body; there would be no light in those dear eyes, no voice to answer her when she called.

To her amazement, the stone which had been rolled before the entrance had been taken away. The dark cavity was unprotected. She dare not look within. She turned and ran back to tell some one! The first

she met were Peter and John. What could it mean?
The woman cried distractedly, 'They have taken Him
away,' and the two disciples, without argument, ran
to learn the truth for themselves. She followed
them, and saw them coming out from the tomb and
its emptiness. No wonder that they rushed by,
scarcely seeing her. They must tell the others of this
deserted grave. For a moment she stood alone,
weeping. Then she gathered new courage, drew
near the tomb, and stooped beneath the arching rock
to enter. Her heart stopped beating, then seemed to
break, in one last agony. The place was empty; even
the Body had gone. She had nothing left at all—
nothing but her memories. The storm had its way
with her. This was the end.

Blinded by her tears, she stumbled on. The early
morning light was wakening the flowers; they had
only been asleep, but He was dead. Even His body
had been taken away!

In the distance a figure was coming towards her.
He was a gardener, doubtless. Perhaps it was he who
had removed the body, lest his flowers should be
trampled by the feet of the mourners coming to the
tomb.

Her thoughts were confused. Some one had
spoken to her from the emptiness as she stood by the
road. She seemed to remember the Shining Ones
asking her why she wept. She had told them she had
lost her Lord. But why had she not asked them
where His body had been taken? Here was the

gardener, now. She could ask him, but as her lips began to frame the question, he spoke.

'Woman, why weepest thou?' he said. 'Whom are you seeking?'

She looked through a mist of tears and forgot his question. 'Sir, if thou hast borne him hence, tell me where thou hast laid him, and I will take him away.'

Then He said to her, 'Mary'. Suddenly she knew! No tears could blind her, no tempestuous sorrow could shut her off from this revelation. She knew, but not because He had proclaimed Himself. 'Thou art Mary,' He said; not 'I am Jesus.' That was why she was so sure. No one else could speak her name like that. 'My Master,' she cried and fell at His feet in joy unspeakable. It was she who had been lost, not Jesus.

Long ago, when she had seemed devil-possessed, He had brought peace to her tormented soul. Now once more there came into her broken heart the healing of His love. Yet He had only spoken her name. 'Thou art Mary.' What less could He have said? What more? It was enough. She knew herself and she recognized her risen Lord.

The storm had passed—or was it that its wild winds had blended in a song of life, the spring song of a soul that had found its bearings?

Many a year afterwards on the cotton-fields of Alabama other women entered into the joy of deliverance. They were slaves no more. They sang, in ecstasy, as only they can sing for whom new life begins:

> There's a li'l wheel a-turnin' in ma heart;
> There's a li'l wheel a-turnin' in ma heart.
>   In ma heart, in ma heart,
> There's a li'l wheel a-turnin' in ma heart.

So in the heart of Mary, that first Easter Day, was born a song of new life which no storm could ever silence. It all began because Jesus had identified her! In the storm she had found herself.

I

The process of identification is the more difficult because we do not always realize our own necessity. It is so easy to get lost amidst the maze of things— easiest of all when the storm seems to blot out the ancient landmarks and to sweep away the old familiar things.

The wise men tell us their secrets and we are put in our proper places. Yesterday a man could go out and look at the quiet stars in wonder, but in peace. To-day he is warned that they are vast worlds tearing across the mystery that is space, and covering incredible distances. Great telescopes reveal new immensities, and man cowers in fearful insignificance. Even his most terrible engines of war look like the stupid playthings of a malevolent midget. Space has become wider than our minds can comprehend. We stagger on our tiny plot and lose ourselves.

They tell us that man's expectation of life has lengthened, but even as we begin to be pleasantly interested we realize that our three score years and ten are relatively much shorter than we imagined. Time has been pushed back. We look at the shell of a tiny fresh-water oyster, and are informed that it was made 'about two hundred million years ago'. Whether we accept such astronomic figures or not matters little. We cannot escape the feeling that the few thousand years of human history is as a moment of time and our own mortal life too short to measure. Indeed, we wonder if we should bother to live. We are lost in the unending cycle of the years.

We are lost—but who are we? From the laboratory comes an answer. We are made up of certain elements—oxygen, hydrogen, carbon, phosphorus, sulphur, potassium, iron, and so on. We could be resolved into what could be contained in, shall we say, fifteen medium-sized bottles and stored on a shelf. There is nothing rare or unique about any of them. It is not a flattering description. Once again, if we are satisfied with that, we lose ourselves—and yet there was an 'Ode to a Nightingale', by a young poet, Keats. Was that contained in any or all of the bottles on the shelf? There was a cry from the Cross: 'Father, forgive them for they know not what they do.' All the retorts and laboratories in the world could not originate or contain the love from which

we are nothing, that glory is nothing.' The beasts do not rejoice in the splendour of the sun or the gentle beauty of a starlit sky. They do not thrill to the lisping words of gratitude from the lips of their offspring. They know nothing of the anguish of the mind that seeks for truth, or the heart that loves and strives to serve. The beasts in the meadows at Tintern Abbey were never moved by intimations of immortality. They did not wonder what life meant or whither it might go. These aspirations and ideals, the remorse of conscious failure to attain, the courage of continuance, the desperate anxiety to arrive, the strange, insistent authority of conscience, the haunting sense of ultimate purpose—all these things man knows. When he remembers, he wonders whether he is really lost. The process of identification may begin. He is some one for whom there seems to be a far-off destiny. The sense of ultimate purpose demands a spiritual fulfilment.

My daughter told me recently of a little child, a Brownie. She arrived one day at her pack meeting wearing an air of importance which children sometimes do. Unfortunately, she had not prepared a little task which had been set. 'You see, Brown Owl,' she said by way of explanation, 'I've been so busy—so very busy—with my thoughtings.'

Man, in spite of all the immensities, in spite of the discovery of the nature of his body, has his 'thoughtings'. He seeks an answer to an empty grave, and, more important, he wants to know the reason why the woman's tears are falling, so that she will not be comforted. It is not the mystery of the body that is breaking her heart; it is the absence of her Lord. She is lost without Him.

II

That word 'identification' will not satisfy us if it stand alone. The two disciples could have called the woman by her name, but if Peter or John had said 'Mary' she would still have roamed the garden, disconsolate and lost. When Jesus uttered the word, it had a new significance. It was not mere identification; it was vocation. He did more than remind her of who she was; He stirred within her the new knowledge of all she wanted to be.

When God speaks to us as individuals, He sorts us out from all the débris, so that we may stand upon our feet and live. By that 'naming' we are immediately related. We are not just human beings with an identity; we are children of the Father, and must behave as men worthy of such kinship.

Preaching on one occasion at St. Martin's, Birmingham, I referred to Lord Nelson. I have forgotten in what circumstances. After the service an old man stopped me. He was bent and frail. I do not think life had been very kind to him, but his eyes were shining. 'Lord Nelson,' he said. 'You mentioned Lord Nelson.' 'Yes, I did,' I answered, a little mystified. 'My grandfather held him in his arms as

he died on the *Victory*,' he explained, and his spare
frame quivered with excitement and pride. He was
no longer a nobody. He was linked up with Nelson
and with all our history! He would never be quite
lost, though all the people in the crowded streets
hustled him.

In the garden of sorrow Mary heard her name
spoken by Him in whose heart were gathered all the
sorrows of the world. All her life she would remember it.

> She looked at Him as one who awakes,
> The past was a sleep, and her life began.

To-morrow she would set out to fulfil her charge.
His naming of her was her new commission.

It is because we are capable of hearing and answering such a call that we are perplexed. Beasts that are
fed and sheltered are never conscious of being lost,
but men are not satisfied with food for the body.
There is a hunger of the heart which will not be
denied. Life cannot be limited by its physical neces-
sities and be satisfactory. There is something to be
done beyond eating and drinking. Man's unhappi-
ness is in part the consequence of his greatness. There
is a phrase in the Epistle of St. James: 'a man who sees
his natural face in a glass'. It was Archbishop Benson
who rendered it: 'a man who observeth the face of
his birth in a mirror'. He expounded the whole verse
by declaring that the study of the Bible helps us to
see, as if we looked into a mirror, the man God meant

us to be. When we understand our vocation, when we hear God calling us by name, I think we begin to realize that there *is* a man God wants us to be. The idea of such a divine purpose is more than a mere identification.

Such a call may well come amidst the howling of the storm. Above all the wailing voices that lamented in Mary's heart, that other Voice sounded clear. There could be no mistaking it. She was so sure that it proclaimed the speaker to her. It was not merely Jesus of Nazareth; it was her Lord. His presence demanded new life from *her* that day and all the days that were to be.

It was so with Thomas, as he cried, 'My Lord and my God!' It is so with all who, listening amidst the roar of guns or the sobbing of a broken heart, are called, sorted out from all the rest, by the Risen Lord.

III

Such sense of identification and vocation brings with it new assurance. Before we leave this story, there is one point we must not fail to notice. She supposed Him to be the gardener. It was He who recognized her, not she who recognized Him.

So often we have pondered and grown anxious lest, when we cross the last frontier, to meet again our blessed dead, we might not know them. Here, in this joyous record, is great consolation. We need be anxious no more. *They* will recognize *us*. As we pass over, with the same identity, the same memories above all, the same love—why should we fear? They who have gone before us to the 'Shadowless Land' will make no mistake.

So, then, Mary stepped into a new life. For a moment she did not understand. She would have touched His feet in adoration, but it was not to be. He would come nearer to His friends than ever before. Bodies separate; the spirit unites. He was risen, indeed, and presently they knew He was risen in their hearts. As He appeared to the rest of the disciples, He made it plain that they would no longer see Him or touch Him as of old. He had come to them more intimately; He was theirs beyond all losing now.

Here is joy for you and me. Amongst all the immensities of time and space, amidst all the tragedies past our individual control, in the storm of war itself, we are not lost. He has called us by name. We belong to God. We find our toil and our rest in Him.

2

THE END OF THE PROBLEM

And we know that to them that love God all things work together for good.

ROMANS VIII. 28

be tossed up as driftwood on some distant shore. It would be difficult to imagine, as they lie upon the beach, that they were working. The pitiful relics of a street accident speak tragically of some mistake, but they do not, in themselves, guarantee a final good.

Is it possible, then, to believe in a God who counts where a world is so woefully wrong?

'To them that love God, all things work together for good', says Paul, and the Christian accepts that as a basic fact of his life. What does it mean for him?

It used to be supposed, quite simply, and very selfishly, that God looked after His own, shielding them from all physical harm. There are still those who imagine that Christians should be immune from bombs or similar disasters! But if that were the meaning we should expect to find a sure proof in Paul's own life. On the contrary, he of all men knew the fierceness of the storm. Five times he received forty stripes save one, three times he was beaten with rods, once he was stoned, three times shipwrecked. He spent a day and a night in the deep, he passed through perils of rivers, of robbers, was threatened by Jews and Gentiles, faced death in the city and in the desert, was betrayed, nearly died of hunger and of thirst, starved in the cold, shivered in prison cells and was slain, at last, by a Roman sword. One could scarcely say he enjoyed a sheltered life. If he simply meant that God gives His servants immunity from physical dangers, then his own life is a complete refutation of the theory.

There is another interpretation which developed later. It suggests that the world is steadily progressing. This 'evolutionary optimism', as it has been called, implies that there is no need for any kind of anxiety. Eternal forces are directed towards a splendid goal. One may shut one's ears to the scientist when he declares that the universe is running down and that energy deteriorates. That in itself would be difficult, but one must be deaf, also, to the cry of the wounded and the distressed, as they wonder why God does not intervene to protect them.

Perhaps because such interpretations seemed unreal or impossible, men have turned in recent years to a humanism which proclaims the sufficiency of the creative and redemptive forces within themselves. These, we are urged to believe, will ensure that all things work together for good. Man can dispense with God. All the circumstances which distress us—disease, and poverty, war, and every form of criminal activity—are to be ended by man's own effort. By increasing his knowledge and reforming his social and economic system, he is going to advance to new heights and happiness. He is able to build a brave, new world. So much for the theory; but man just does not accept it. He does not believe in himself. He has so often let himself down! Each new discovery has threatened him with new perils. Instead of peace, he has found war. Because he cannot rule himself, he doubts his ability to direct

I

If we are to interpret the words aright, we must concentrate first on that word 'together'. Here is a principle of universal co-operation. Some one has said that the daring of Paul was the logic of Paul. It must be all things or nothing. A summer-time religion is worse than useless. The only faith worth having is one which believes in a God who is Love in every circumstance of human life.

Let us begin here. Man, himself, is part of the natural order. He claims no exemption from its operations. Every man, for example, is subject to the law of gravitation, every man knows physical hunger, and no man is immune from poison. It would be absurd to expect that God made strange exceptions. Even Jesus toiled in climbing the hill from the shore of Galilee. Many a saint has died of hunger. No one dreamed that Socrates would drink the fatal dose of hemlock and live. We are satisfied that these natural laws obtain for all men, irrespective of their creed or morals.

Is it unreasonable to suggest that the inviolability of the laws make for man's safety and happiness? It is true that water may drown a man, but it is true also that the combination of hydrogen and oxygen which we call water is one of the means by which he lives. The sea has hidden a thousand thousand wrecks, and been the grave of many a human body, but the sea is also a great cradle of life. Water is not merely 'all right' in its place; it is absolutely essential to life. Sometimes through ignorance or faulty judgement, sometimes of set purpose, man breaks or defies a law, jolts things out of place and suffers. The evil result is certainly not part of the Divine order; it is rather the consequence of human disorder.

At the same time, it is obvious that even when such suffering is part of an educative process there will be those who are, like innocent victims, bearing pain for us who learn. How could it be otherwise? If we were puppets moved by some unseen actor, we might escape some dangers, but we should remain puppets, not men.

The divine gift of freedom brings with it responsibility. We must learn the laws and keep them.

To expect immunity from some kinds of disaster because we love God would be to desire a strange suspension of the laws which govern the universe. It would involve our accepting unreliability in the whole machinery of life. The laws of God are an essential part of the love of God. When we understand them and obey them, we realize the divine harmony. There is no discord in the heart of God, and evil is not part of the divine order.

In the private papers of the Tolstoy family there is a charming incident related by Count Leo's eldest son, Sergius. His little brother Ilya had received a beautiful cup and saucer from the Christmas Tree in the great hall at Yasnaya Polyana. He was delighted with his present and, clutching it in his tiny hands, rely on that light when sunset brought the end of the day and the end of his work in the field. Think, too, of the adventures of the Book, of man's first attempts to write, of his struggle to catch the whisper of God's voice, of the long, laborious copying of script—these and countless other things have made the homely scene possible. Man has begun to learn the physical laws of his world. He has begun to learn other and higher laws of mind and spirit, so that he can harness the material. There, in the little cottage, God is working things together for his child. That is no creation of fancy; it is simple fact.

It is also true that to the little village, not long ago, they carried the bodies of four educated men, masters at a great public school. They had met their deaths in an avalanche in the mountains. It was not so much that they consciously disobeyed laws as that they did not obey them, but it would be foolish to say this proves God does not work!

Somewhere, at the heart of all these infinite complexities, stands Love. In spite of all man's dullness and stupidity, He waits patient yet eager to continue His work, even with broken pieces. Can we rely on Him?

How often we come, as one came a century ago to Abraham Lincoln, crying, 'Yes, but is God on our side?' Lincoln answered: 'Sir, I have never yet asked myself whether God was on my side. But I tell you what, sir, I am determined to be on God's side.'

There we reach the heart of our problem.

III

Here we come to what might be called the crisis of understanding. 'And we know that *to them that love God* all things work together for good.' There is no immunity from physical danger guaranteed as a return for our love. It is a much more important thing. Our love releases God's love. As we understand this, the whole situation changes. We may even be staring at the little body that no longer moves, but we shall be able to see beyond into the heavenly places. We shall know that this tragedy was not the end—it was not even the end of one of God's sentences.

I remember, as a boy, learning from an old Latin grammar. In one chapter there was an example of the subjective and objective genitive. It stood a little strangely in that commonplace book:

Amor Dei, the love of God, i.e. the love which we have for God or the love which God has for us.

As I sat in the old class-room, 'detained' because I had not learnt the lesson, I stared at the words and wondered just what they meant. I do not know all they mean now. As I strove with the problem of the drowned bairn, I learnt a little more of what they might mean. The love of God to me must somehow be related to my love to Him. In that relationship lay the secret of understanding.

To them that love God all things will become